ULTIMATE GALACTUS
ULTIMATE SECRET

WRITER: **WARREN ELLIS**
PENCILS: **STEVE McNIVEN**
& TOM RANEY

INKS: **MARK MORALES & SCOTT HANNA**
COLORS: **MORRY HOLLOWELL & ROB SCHWAGER**
LETTERS: **CHRIS ELIOPOULOS**
ASSISTANT EDITORS: **JOHN BARBER &**
NICOLE WILEY
ASSOCIATE EDITOR: **NICK LOWE**
EDITOR: **RALPH MACCHIO**

COLLECTION EDITOR: **JENNIFER GRÜNWALD**
ASSISTANT EDITOR: **MICHAEL SHORT**
SENIOR EDITOR, SPECIAL PROJECTS:
JEFF YOUNGQUIST
DIRECTOR OF SALES: **DAVID GABRIEL**
PRODUCTION: **JERRON QUALITY COLOR**
CREATIVE DIRECTOR: **TOM MARVELLI**

EDITOR IN CHIEF: **JOE QUESADA**
PUBLISHER: **DAN BUCKLEY**

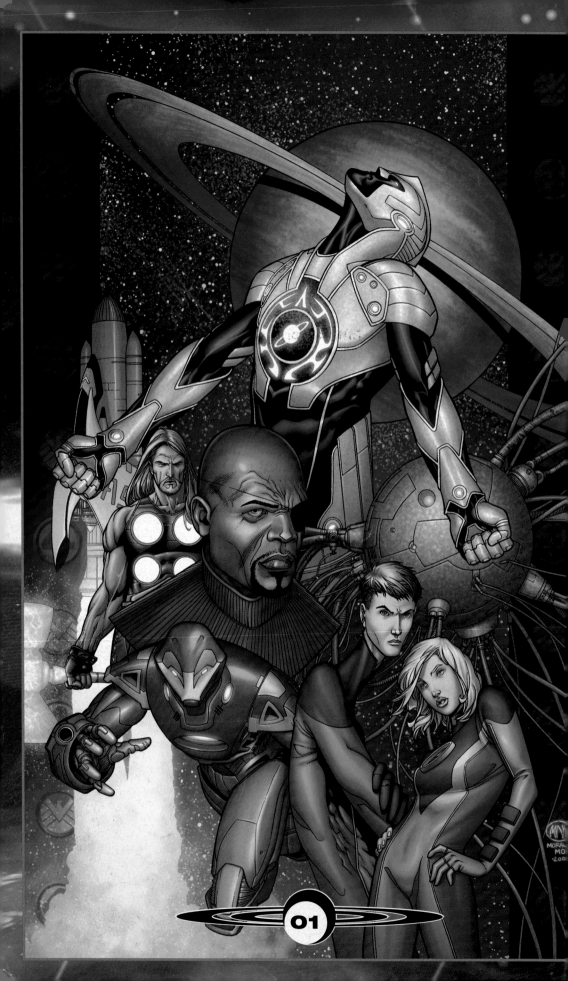

Formed by General Nick Fury and led by Captain America, THE ULTIMATES are a small but lethal army created to protect humanity against all the new rising threats to the world.

The genetic structures of the four super-powered teenagers known as the Fantastic Four were scrambled and recombined in a fantastically strange way. Reed's body stretches and flows like water. Ben looks like a thing carved from desert rock. Sue can become invisible. Johnny generates flame.

NANUET PUBLIC LIBRARY
149 CHURCH STREET
NANUET, NEW YORK 10954
845-623-4281

The events in this story occur before those in our companion title ULTIMATES 2.

Stan Lee presents:

ULTIMATE SECRET

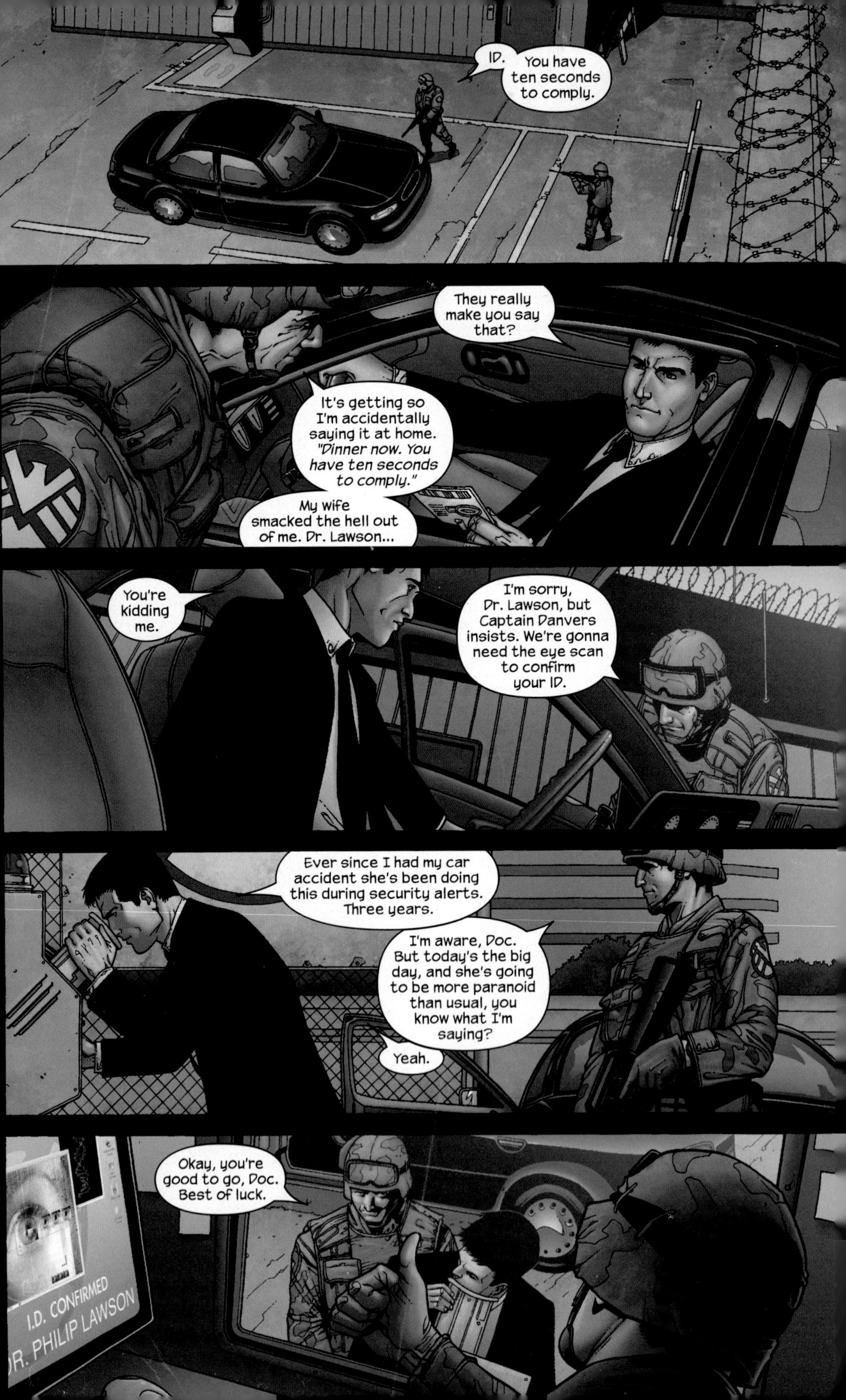
ID.
You have ten seconds to comply.
They really make you say that?
It's getting so I'm accidentally saying it at home. "Dinner now. You have ten seconds to comply."
My wife smacked the hell out of me. Dr. Lawson...
You're kidding me.
I'm sorry, Dr. Lawson, but Captain Danvers insists. We're gonna need the eye scan to confirm your ID.
Ever since I had my car accident she's been doing this during security alerts. Three years.
I'm aware, Doc. But today's the big day, and she's going to be more paranoid than usual, you know what I'm saying?
Yeah.
Okay, you're good to go, Doc. Best of luck.
I.D. CONFIRMED
DR. PHILIP LAWSON

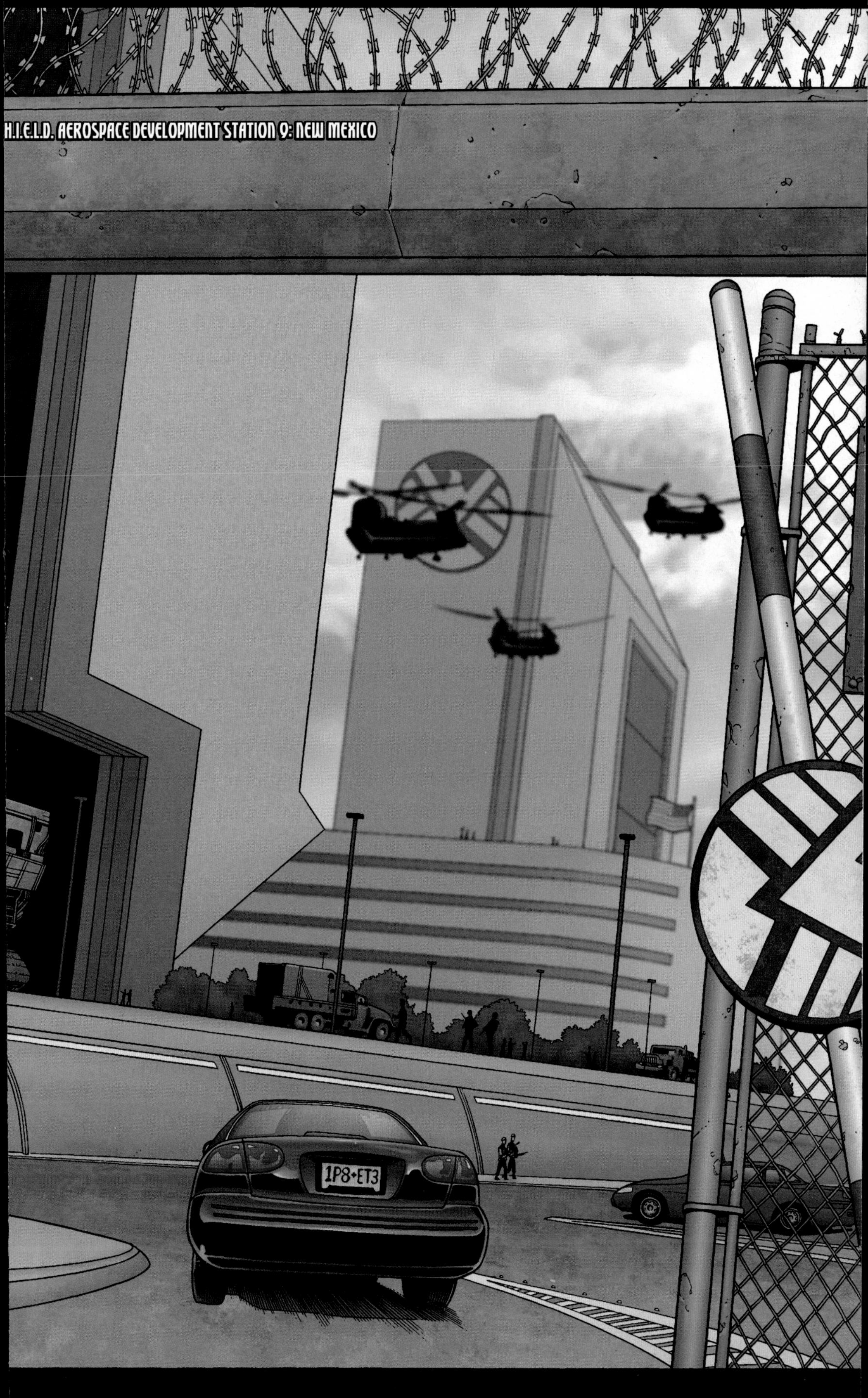
H.I.E.L.D. AEROSPACE DEVELOPMENT STATION 9: NEW MEXICO
1P8+ET3

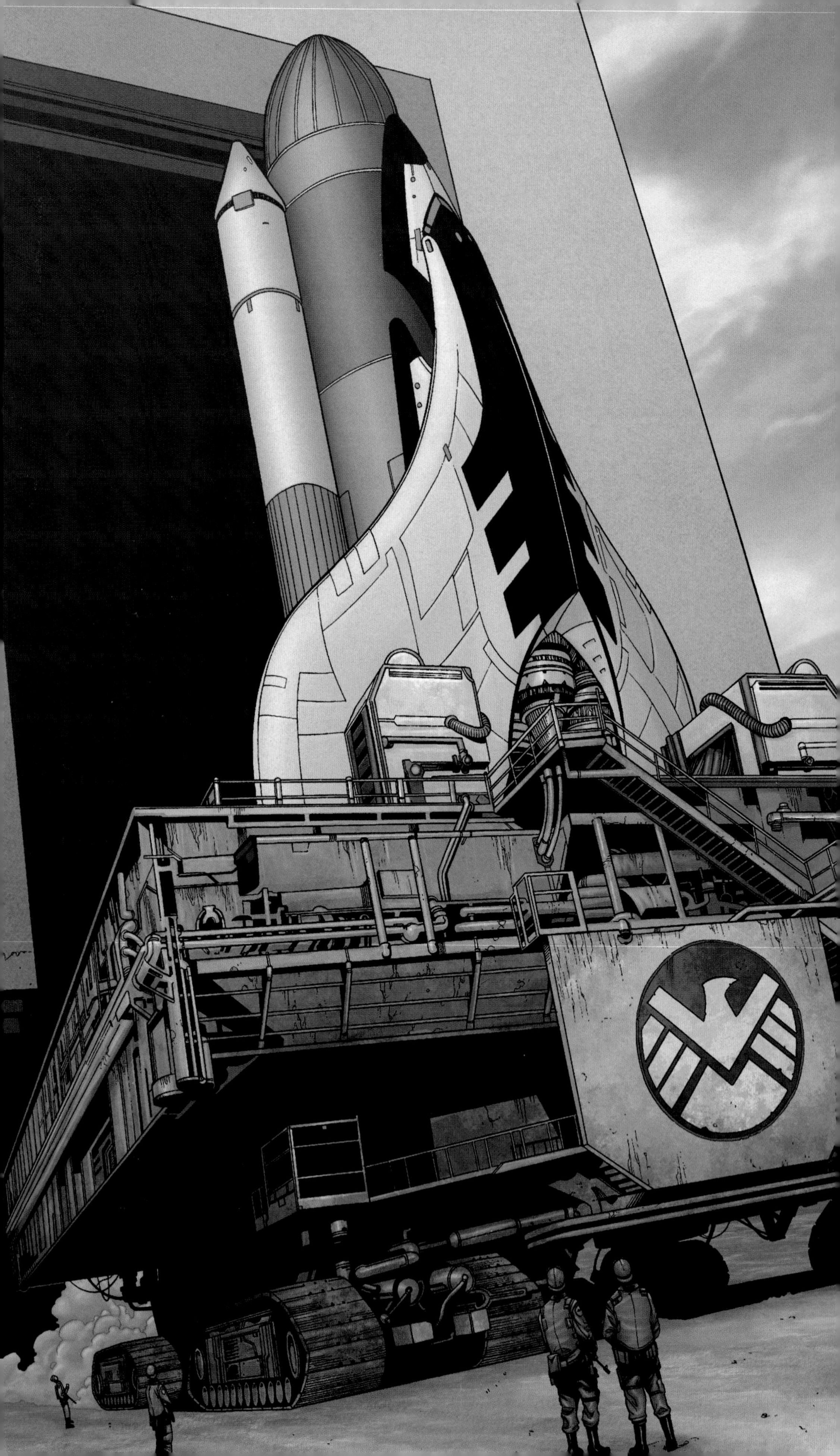

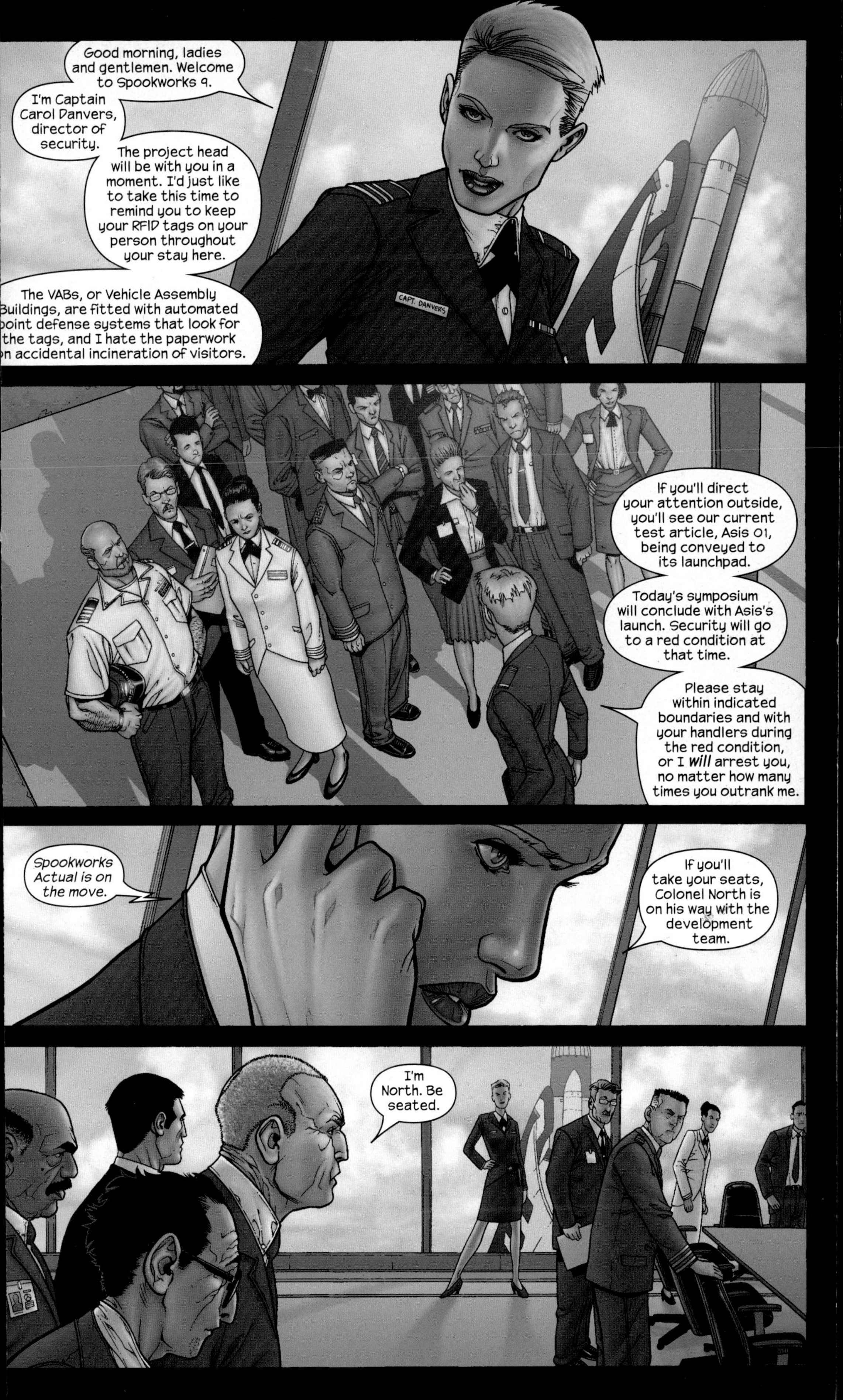
Good morning, ladies and gentlemen. Welcome to Spookworks 9.
I'm Captain Carol Danvers, director of security.
The project head will be with you in a moment. I'd just like to take this time to remind you to keep your RFID tags on your person throughout your stay here.
The VABs, or Vehicle Assembly Buildings, are fitted with automated point defense systems that look for the tags, and I hate the paperwork on accidental incineration of visitors.
CAPT. DANVERS
If you'll direct your attention outside, you'll see our current test article, Asis 01, being conveyed to its launchpad.
Today's symposium will conclude with Asis's launch. Security will go to a red condition at that time.
Please stay within indicated boundaries and with your handlers during the red condition, or I *will* arrest you, no matter how many times you outrank me.
Spookworks Actual is on the move.
If you'll take your seats, Colonel North is on his way with the development team.
I'm North. Be seated.

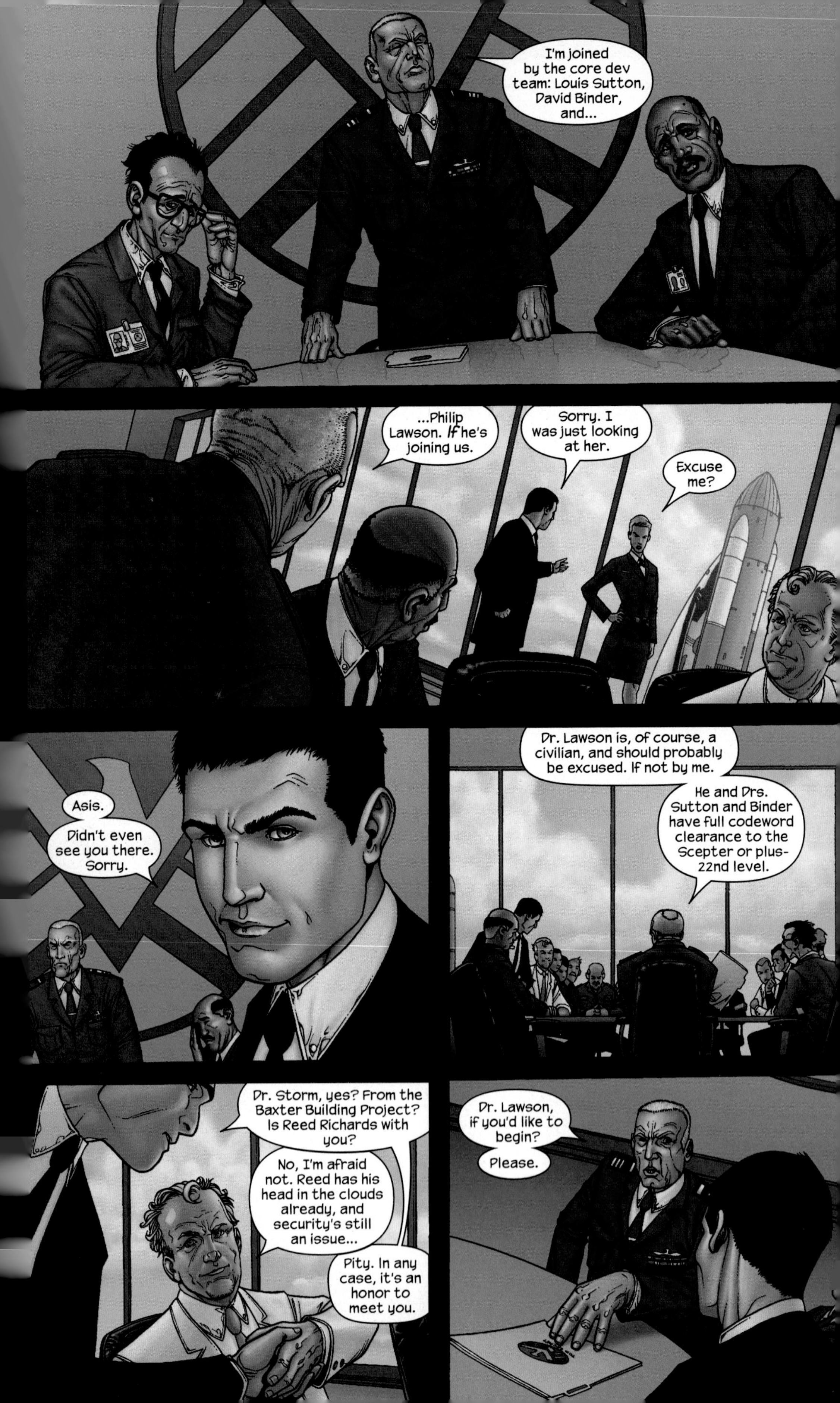

I'm joined by the core dev team: Louis Sutton, David Binder, and...
...Philip Lawson. If he's joining us.
Sorry. I was just looking at her.
Excuse me?
Asis.
Didn't even see you there. Sorry.
Dr. Lawson is, of course, a civilian, and should probably be excused. If not by me.
He and Drs. Sutton and Binder have full codeword clearance to the Scepter or plus-22nd level.
Dr. Storm, yes? From the Baxter Building Project? Is Reed Richards with you?
No, I'm afraid not. Reed has his head in the clouds already, and security's still an issue...
Pity. In any case, it's an honor to meet you.
Dr. Lawson, if you'd like to begin?
Please.

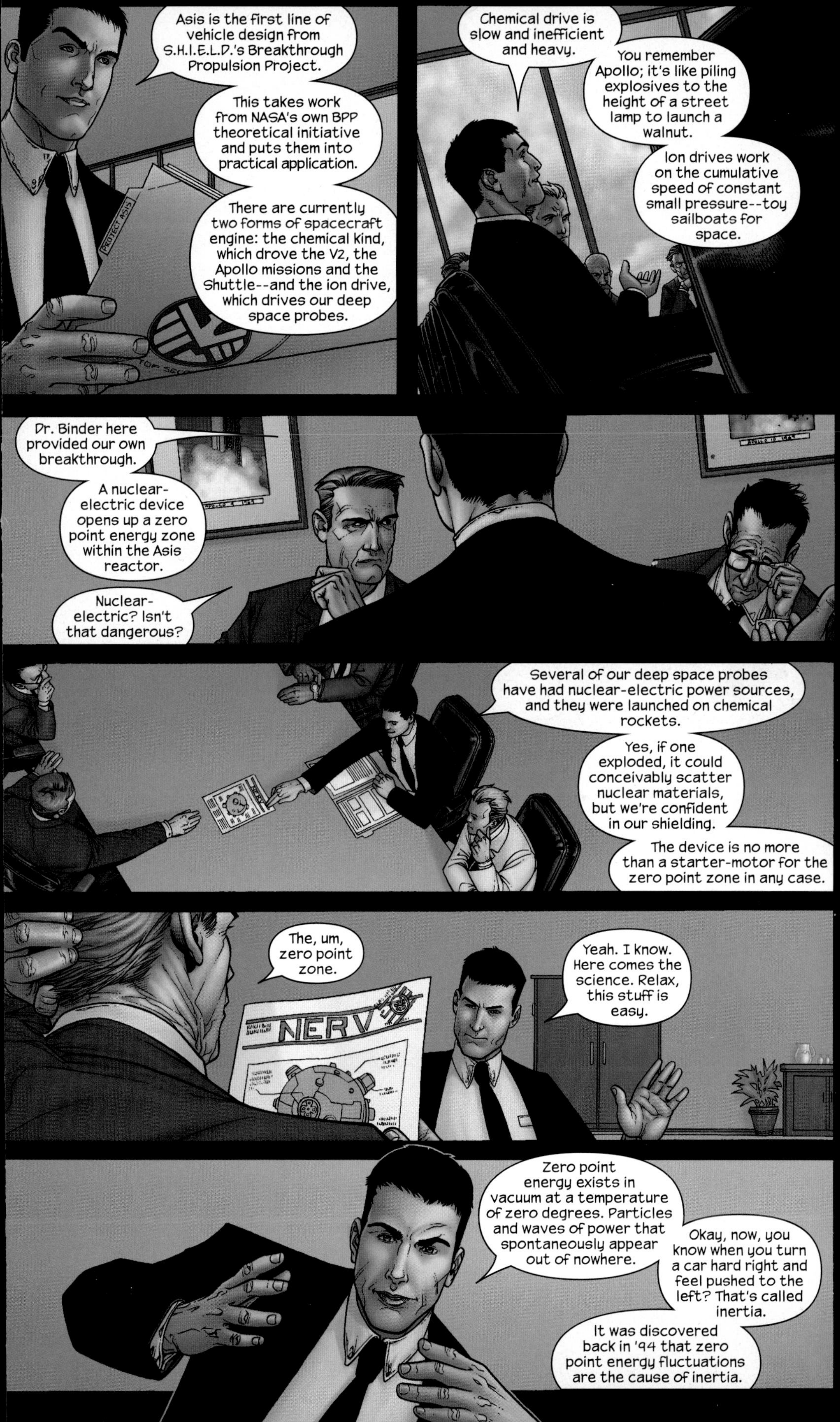

Asis is the first line of vehicle design from S.H.I.E.L.D.'s Breakthrough Propulsion Project.
This takes work from NASA's own BPP theoretical initiative and puts them into practical application.
There are currently two forms of spacecraft engine: the chemical kind, which drove the V2, the Apollo missions and the Shuttle--and the ion drive, which drives our deep space probes.
PROJECT ASIS
Chemical drive is slow and inefficient and heavy.
You remember Apollo; it's like piling explosives to the height of a street lamp to launch a walnut.
Ion drives work on the cumulative speed of constant small pressure--toy sailboats for space.
Dr. Binder here provided our own breakthrough.
A nuclear-electric device opens up a zero point energy zone within the Asis reactor.
Nuclear-electric? Isn't that dangerous?
Several of our deep space probes have had nuclear-electric power sources, and they were launched on chemical rockets.
Yes, if one exploded, it could conceivably scatter nuclear materials, but we're confident in our shielding.
The device is no more than a starter-motor for the zero point zone in any case.
The, um, zero point zone.
Yeah. I know. Here comes the science. Relax, this stuff is easy.
NERV
Zero point energy exists in vacuum at a temperature of zero degrees. Particles and waves of power that spontaneously appear out of nowhere.
Okay, now, you know when you turn a car hard right and feel pushed to the left? That's called inertia.
It was discovered back in '94 that zero point energy fluctuations are the cause of inertia.

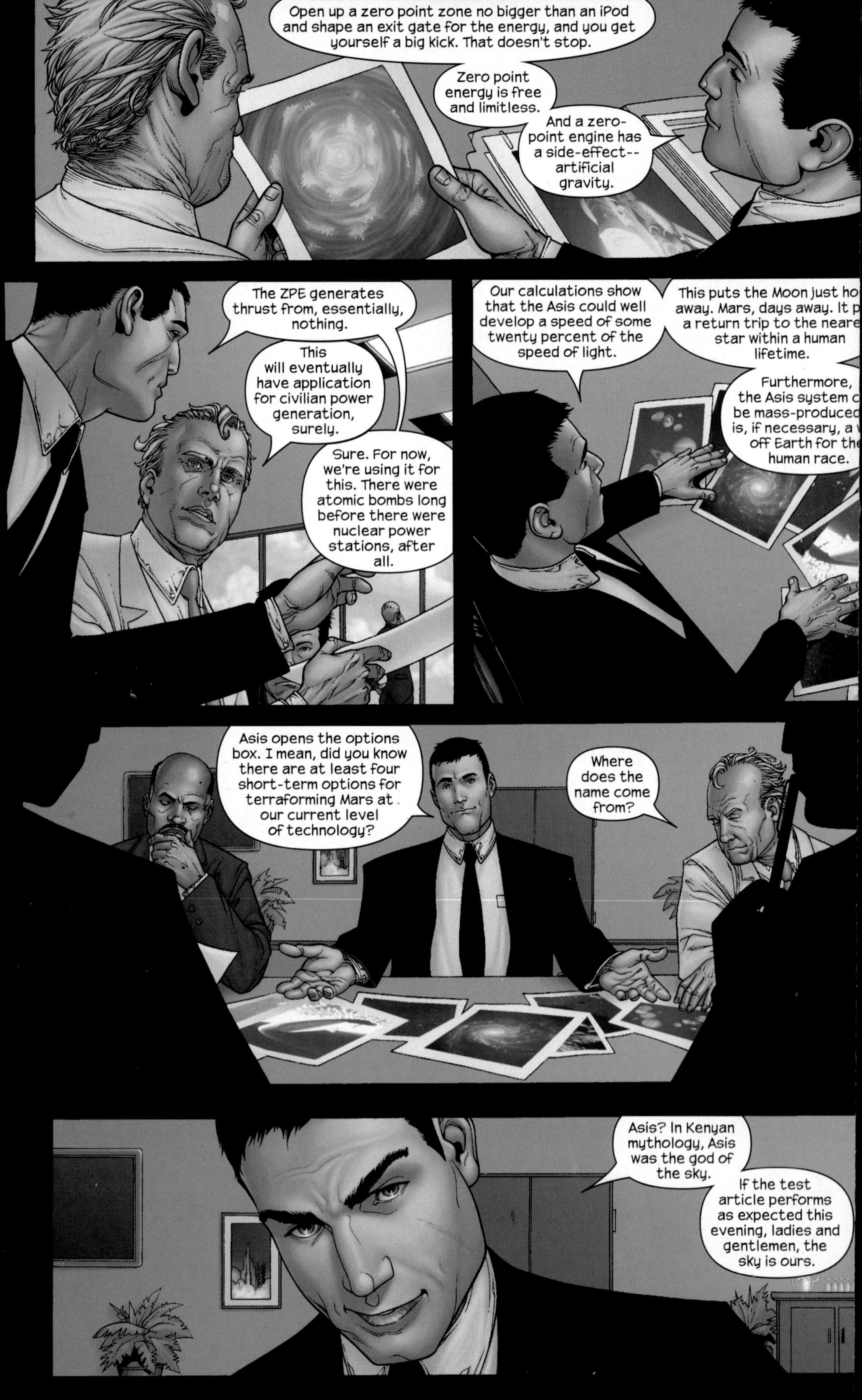
Open up a zero point zone no bigger than an iPod and shape an exit gate for the energy, and you get yourself a big kick. That doesn't stop.
Zero point energy is free and limitless.
And a zero-point engine has a side-effect--artificial gravity.
The ZPE generates thrust from, essentially, nothing.
This will eventually have application for civilian power generation, surely.
Sure. For now, we're using it for this. There were atomic bombs long before there were nuclear power stations, after all.
Our calculations show that the Asis could well develop a speed of some twenty percent of the speed of light.
This puts the Moon just ho away. Mars, days away. It p a return trip to the neare star within a human lifetime.
Furthermore, the Asis system c be mass-produced is, if necessary, a off Earth for the human race.
Asis opens the options box. I mean, did you know there are at least four short-term options for terraforming Mars at our current level of technology?
Where does the name come from?
Asis? In Kenyan mythology, Asis was the god of the sky.
If the test article performs as expected this evening, ladies and gentlemen, the sky is ours.

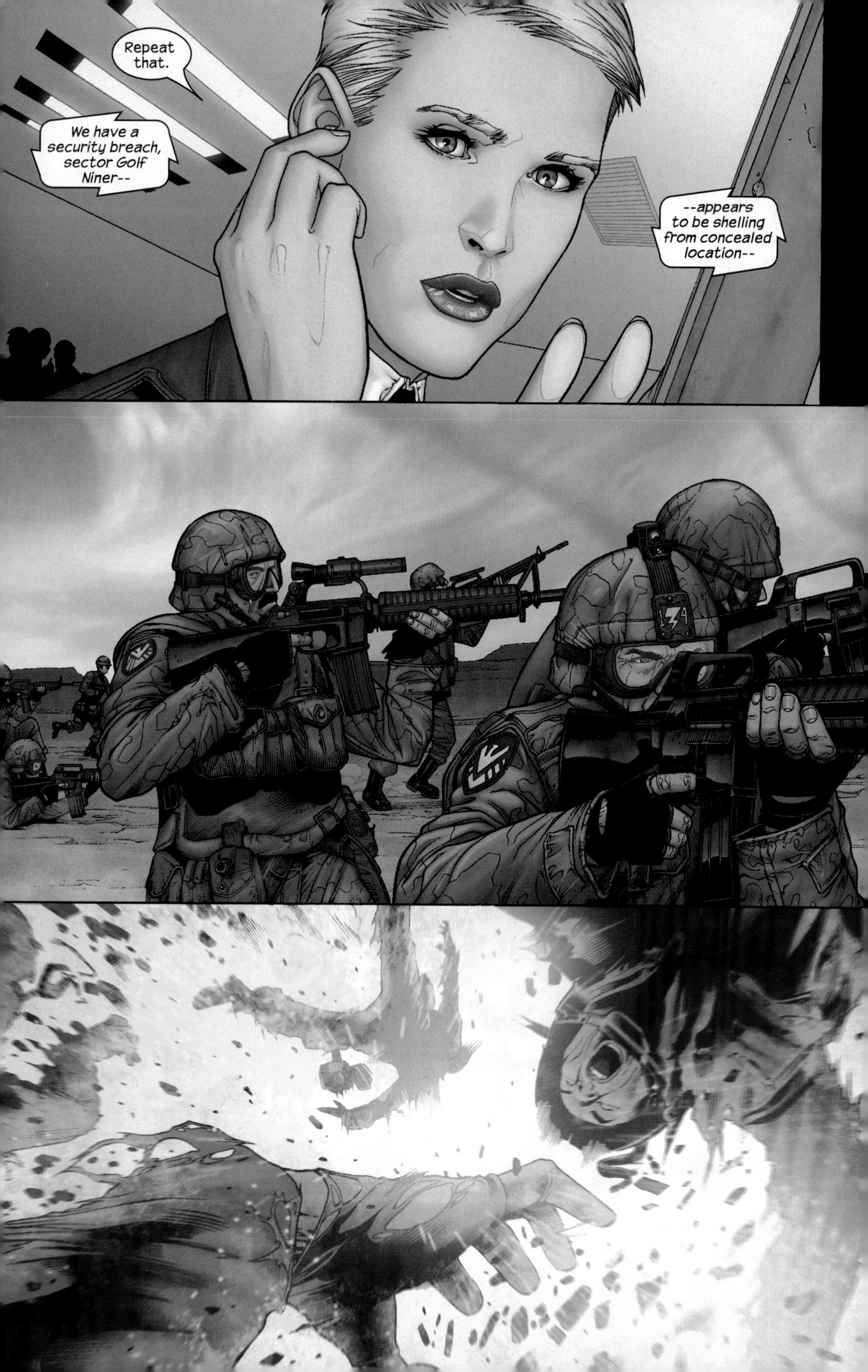
Repeat that.
We have a security breach, sector Golf Niner--
--appears to be shelling from concealed location--

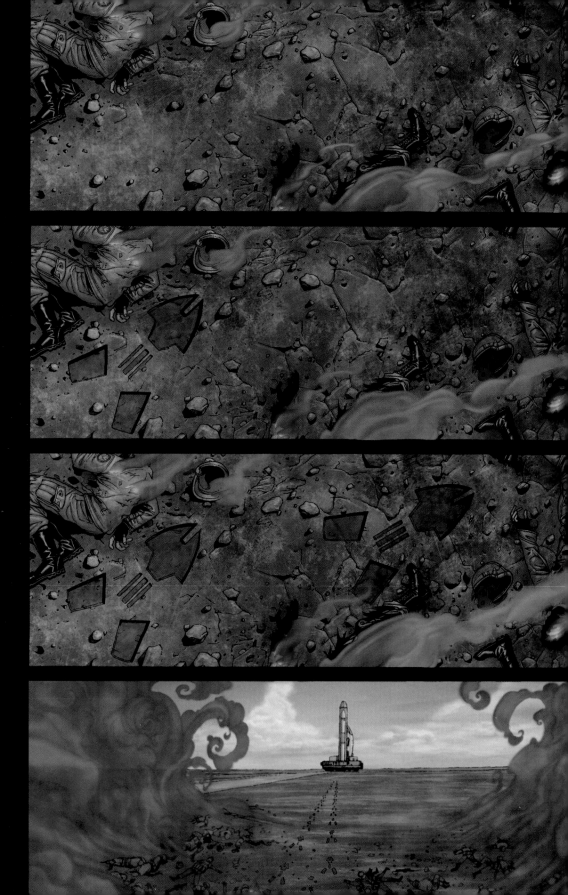

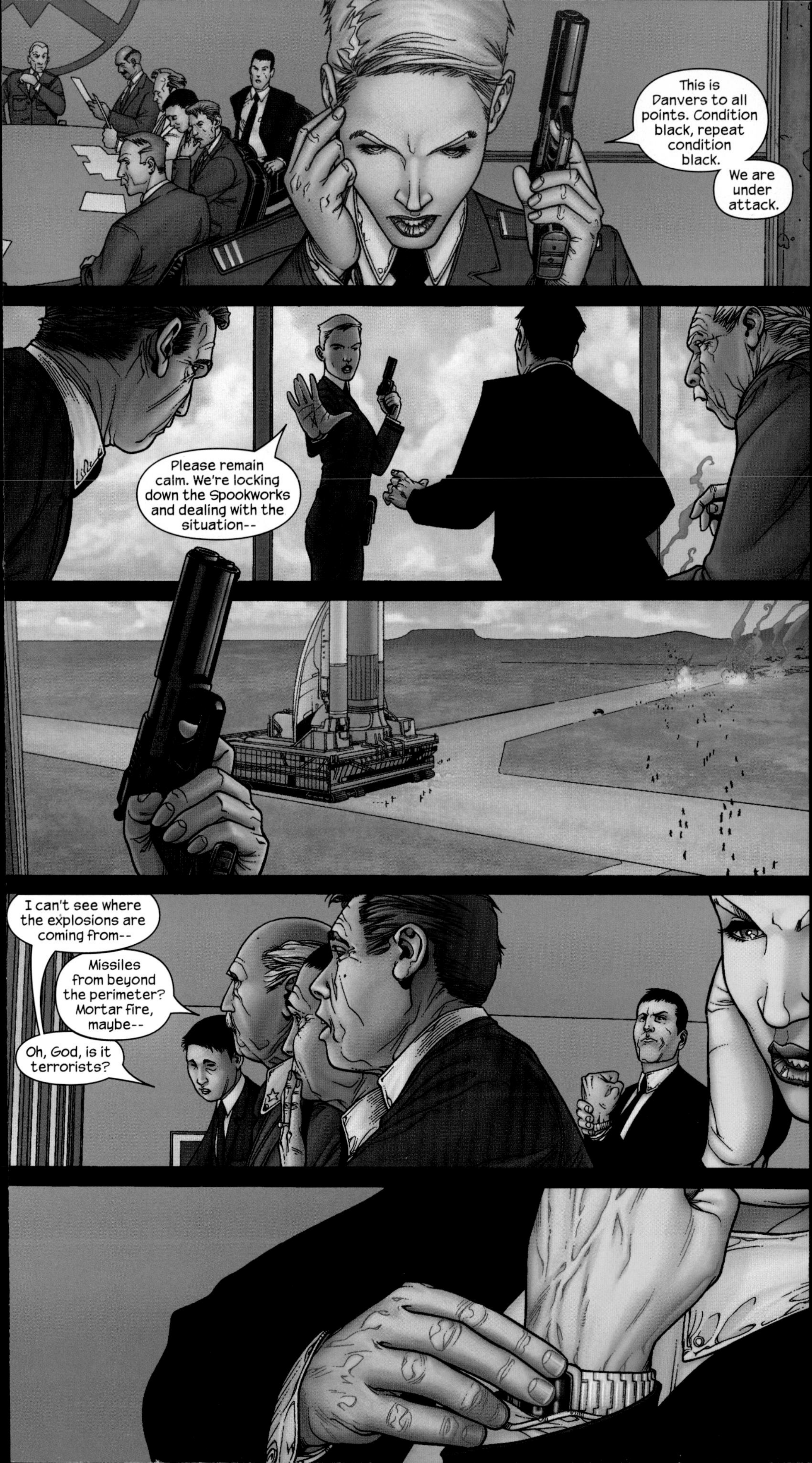
This is Danvers to all points. Condition black, repeat condition black.
We are under attack.
Please remain calm. We're locking down the Spookworks and dealing with the situation--
I can't see where the explosions are coming from--
Missiles from beyond the perimeter? Mortar fire, maybe--
Oh, God, is it terrorists?

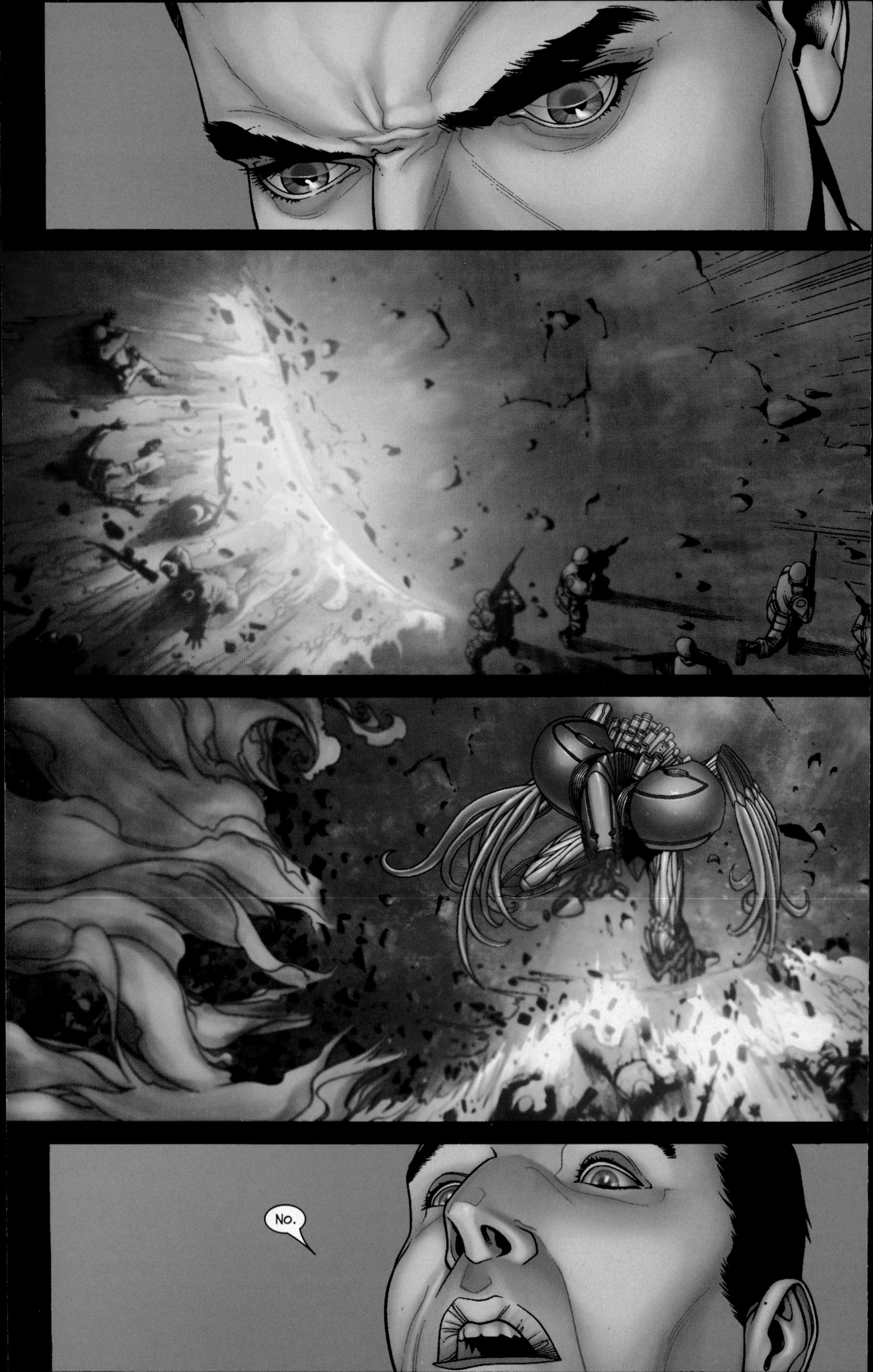
NO.

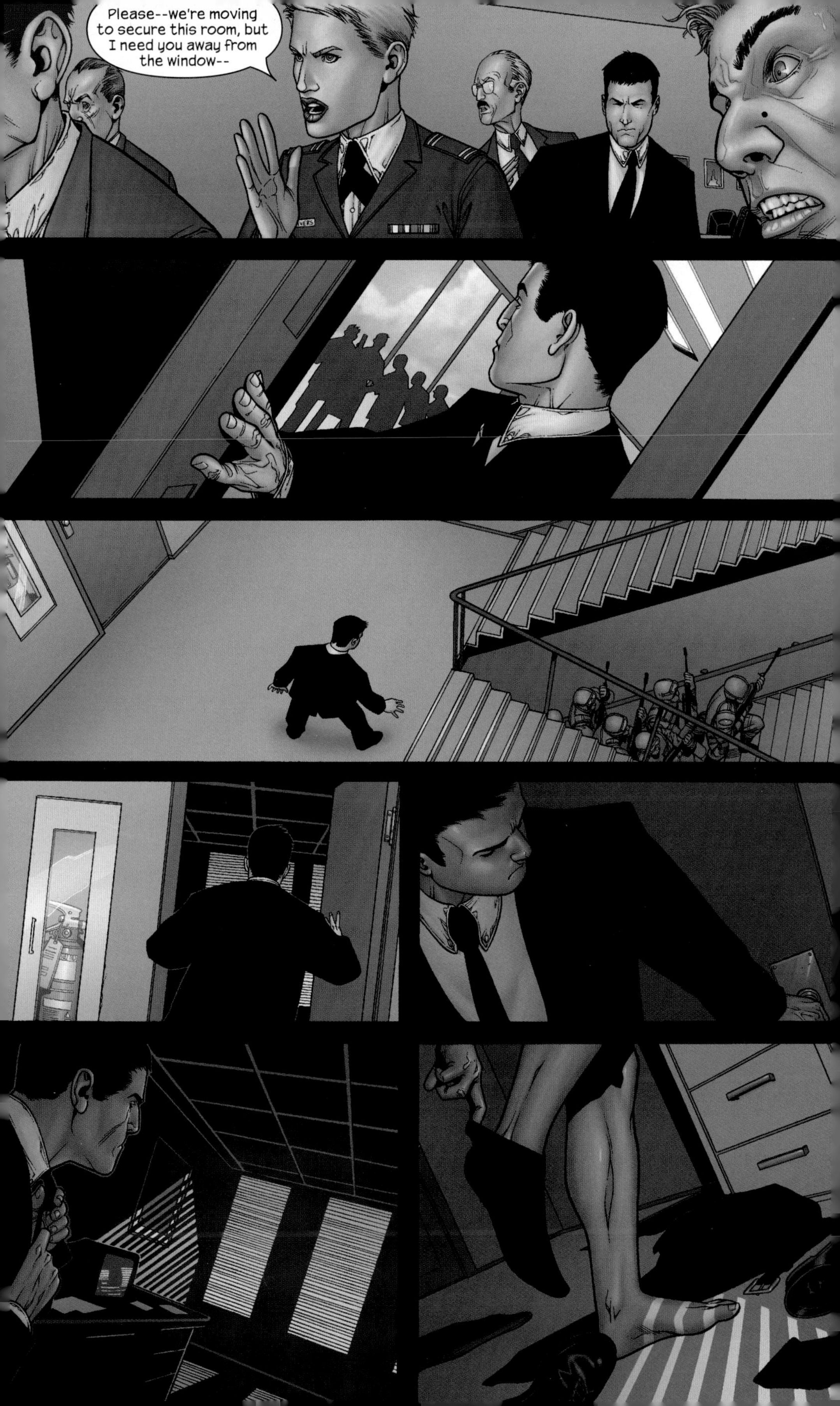
Please--we're moving to secure this room, but I need you away from the window--

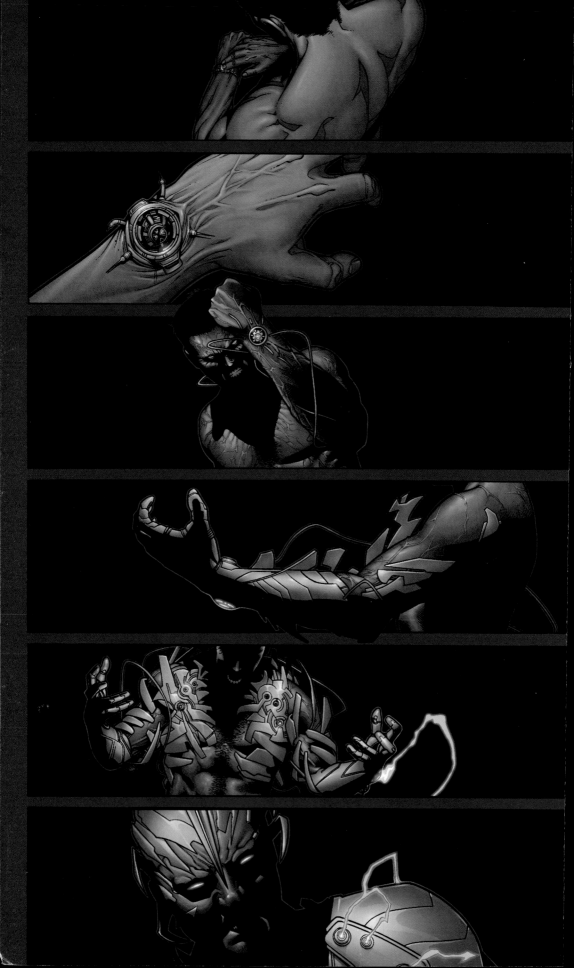

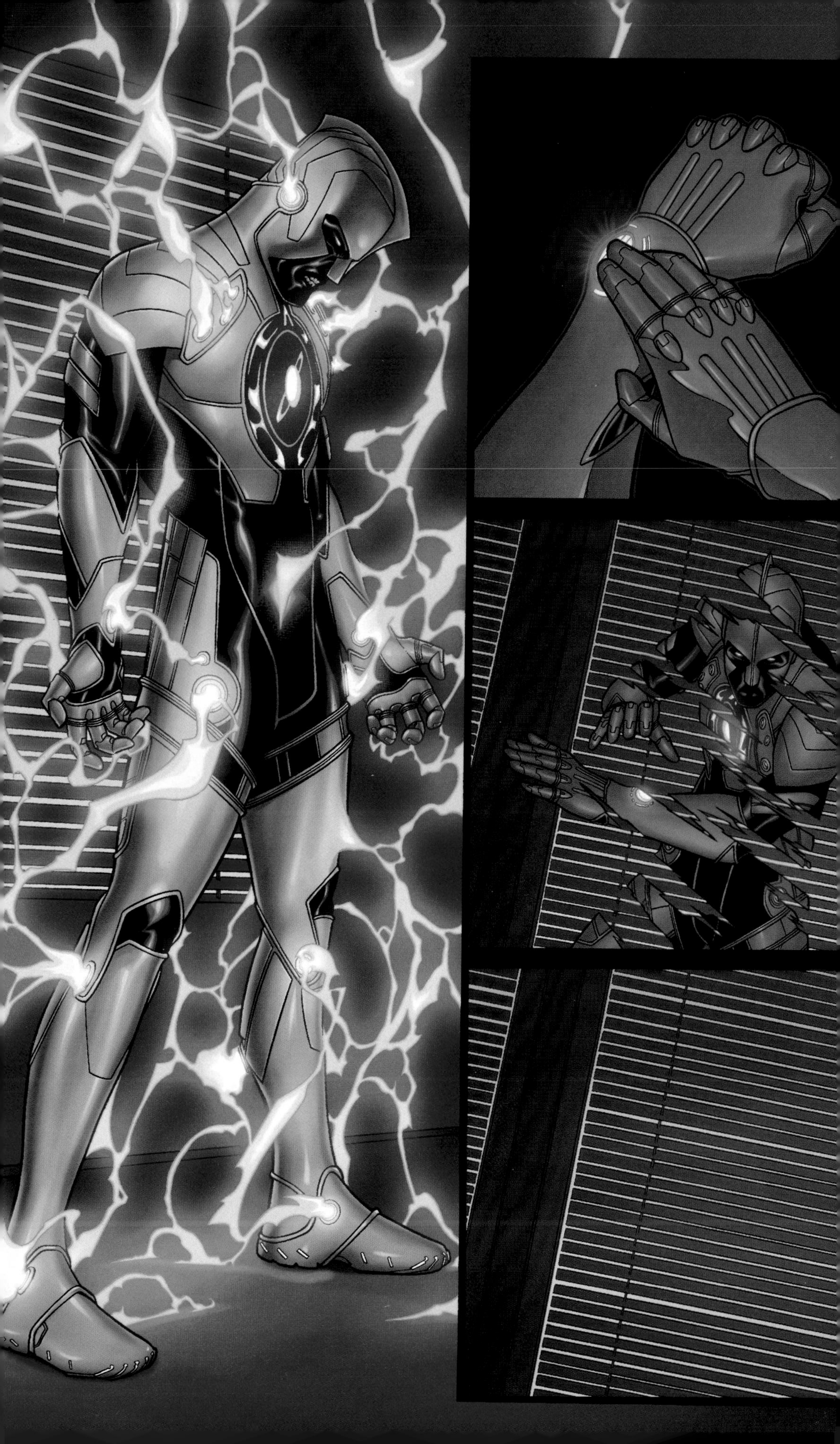

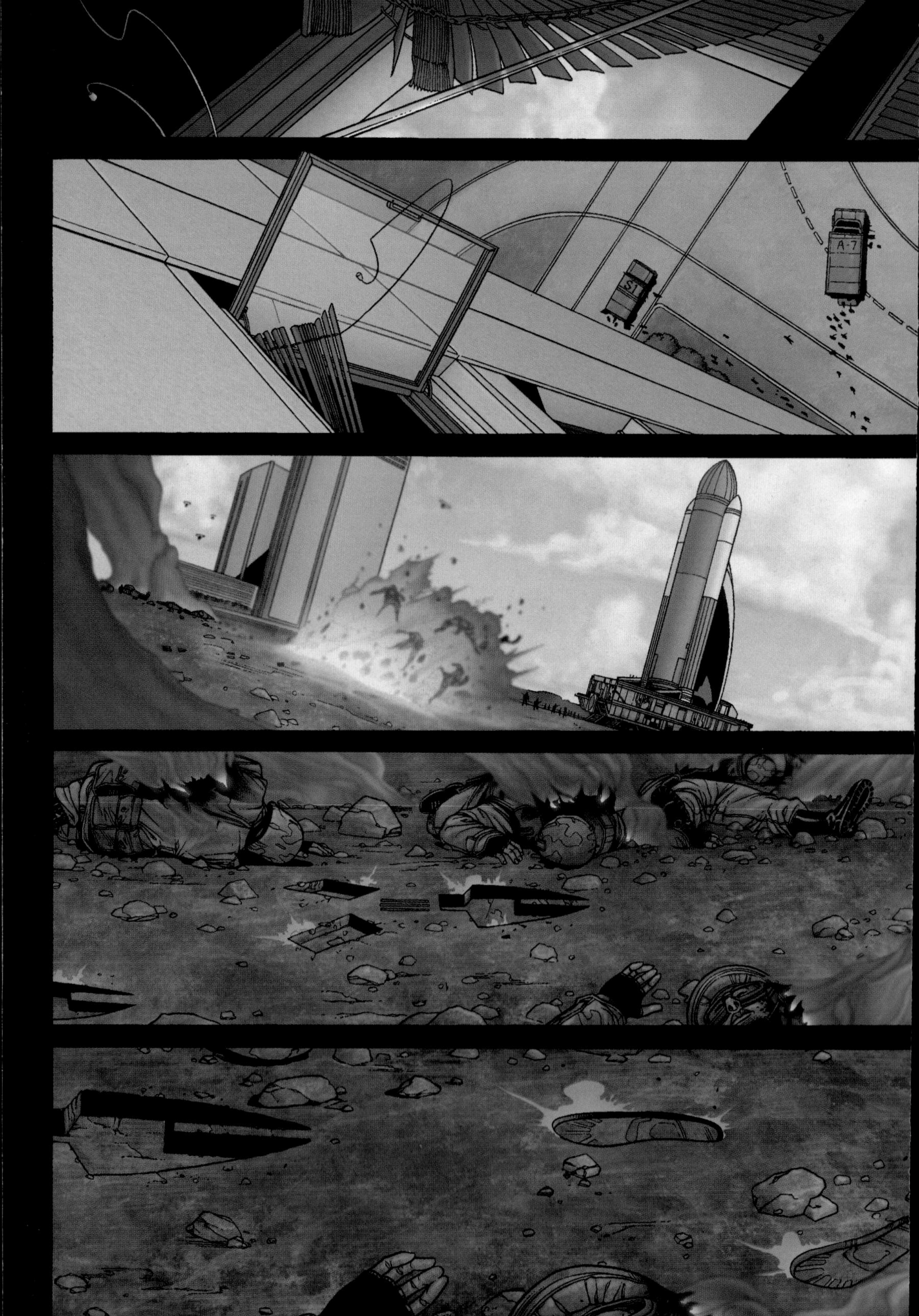
A-7
S1

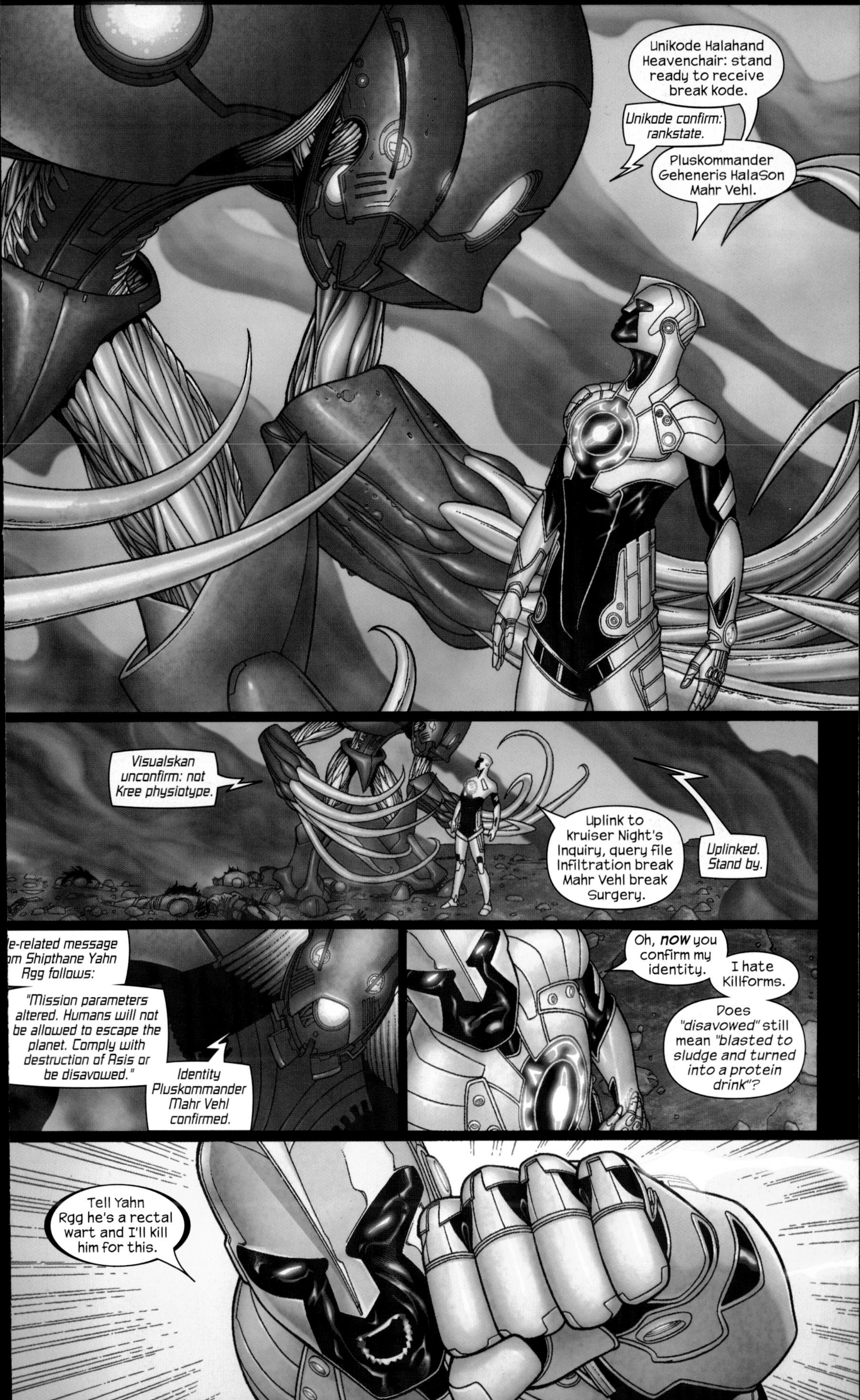
Unikode Halahand Heavenchair: stand ready to receive break kode.
Unikode confirm: rankstate.
Pluskommander Geheneris HalaSon Mahr Vehl.
Visualskan unconfirm: not Kree physiotype.
Uplink to kruiser Night's Inquiry, query file Infiltration break Mahr Vehl break Surgery.
Uplinked. Stand by.
le-related message om Shipthane Yahn Rgg follows:
"Mission parameters altered. Humans will not be allowed to escape the planet. Comply with destruction of Asis or be disavowed."
Identity Pluskommander Mahr Vehl confirmed.
Oh, NOW you confirm my identity.
I hate Killforms.
Does "disavowed" still mean "blasted to sludge and turned into a protein drink"?
Tell Yahn Rgg he's a rectal wart and I'll kill him for this.

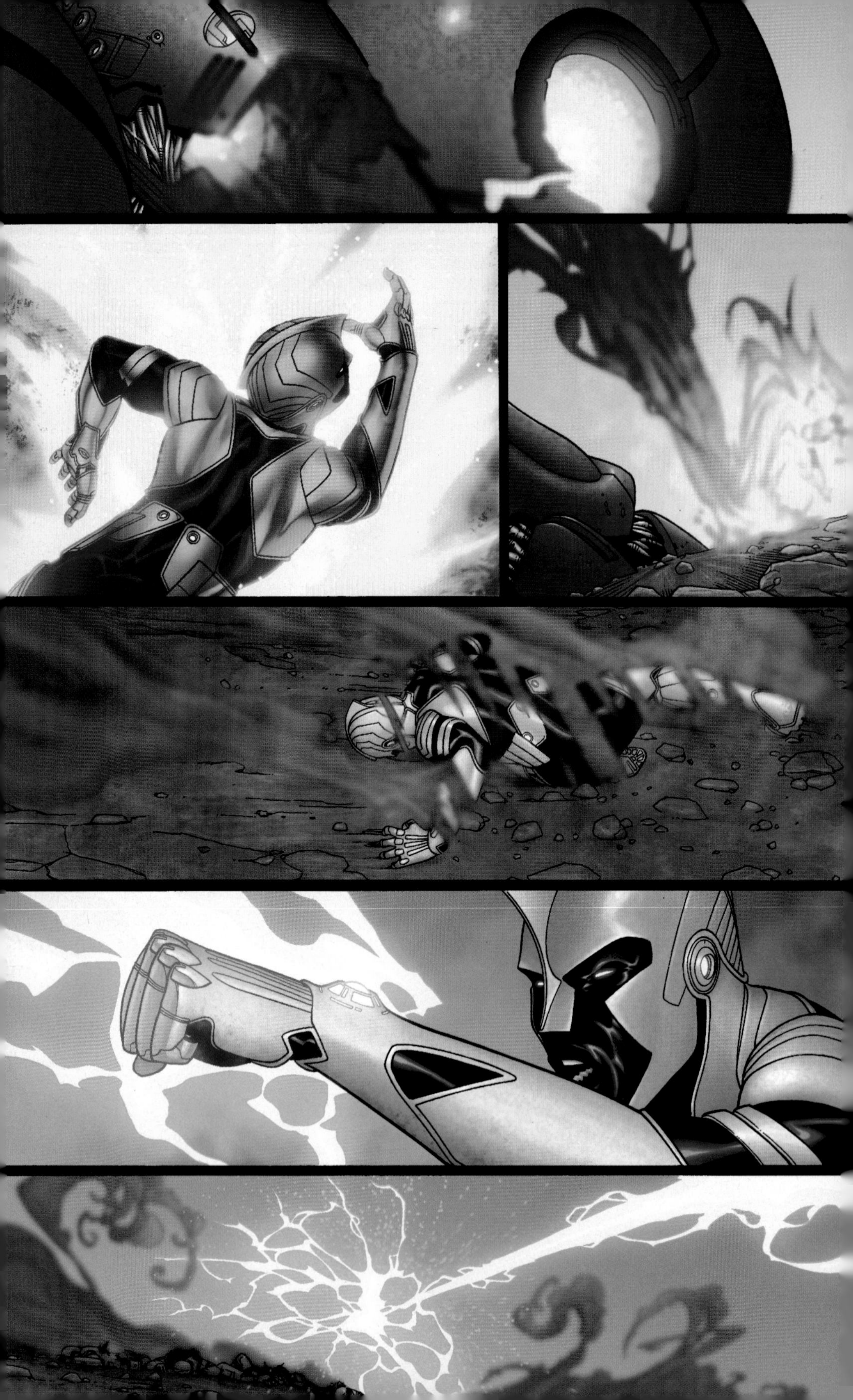

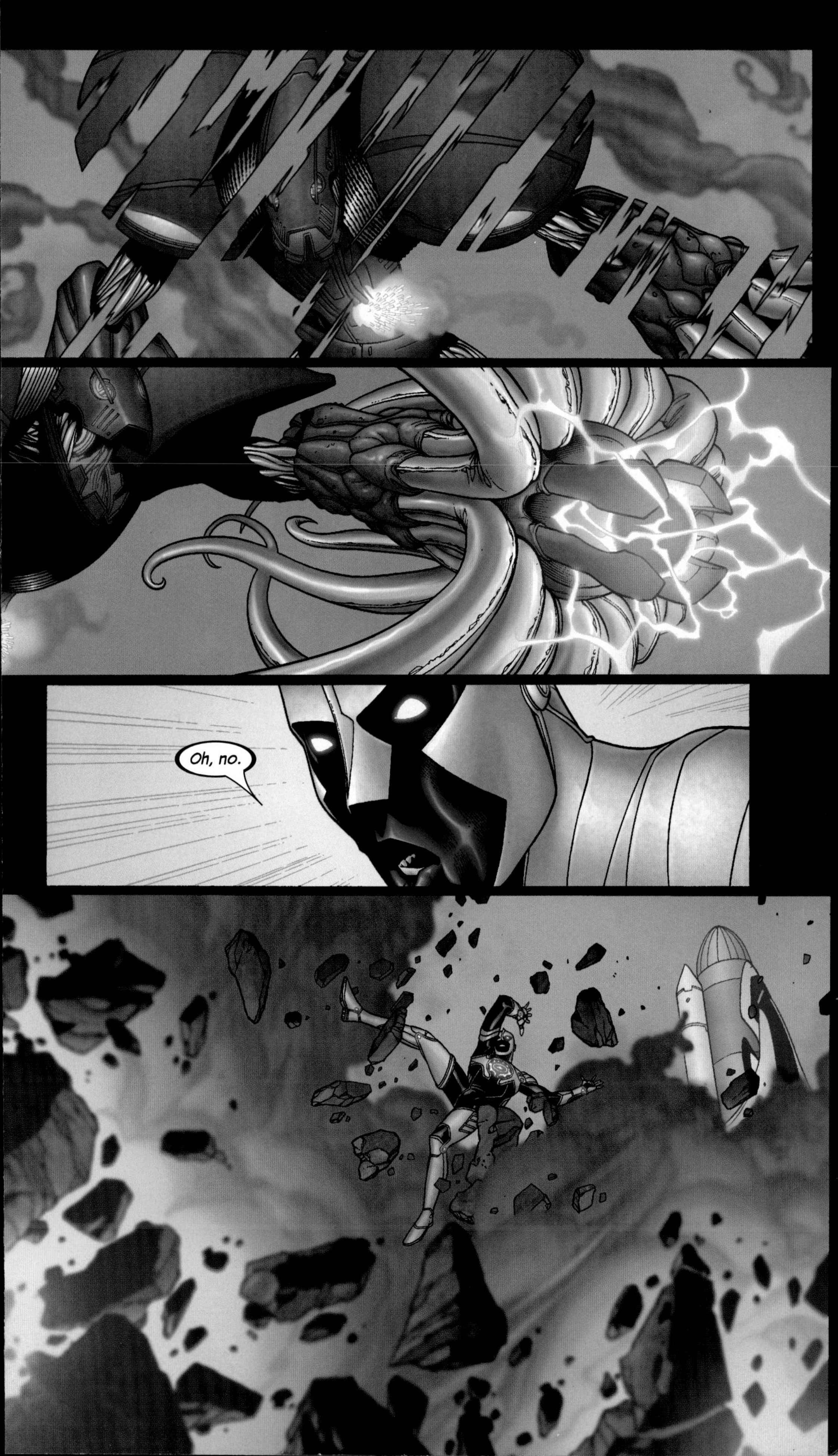
Oh, no.

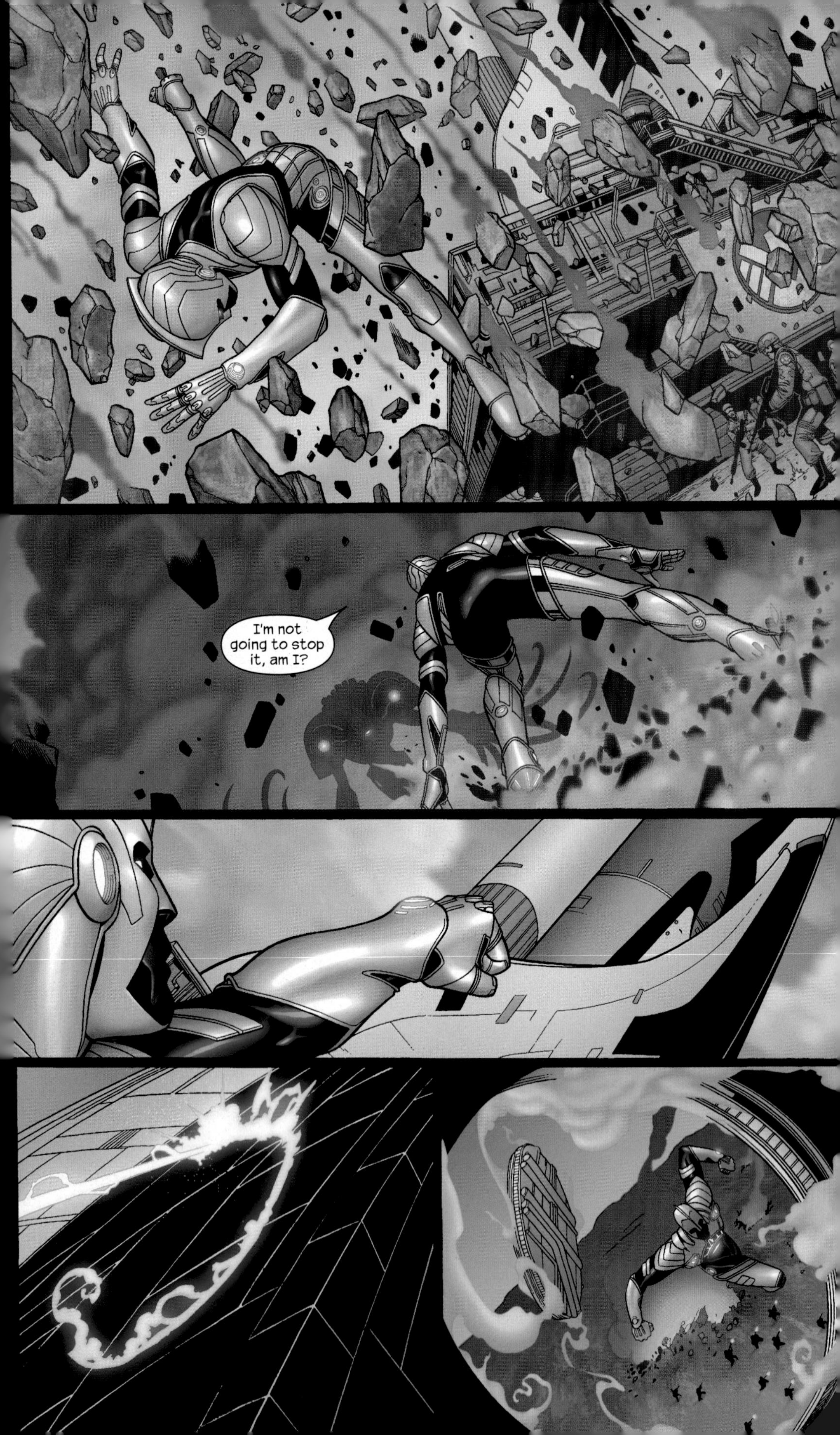
I'm not going to stop it, am I?

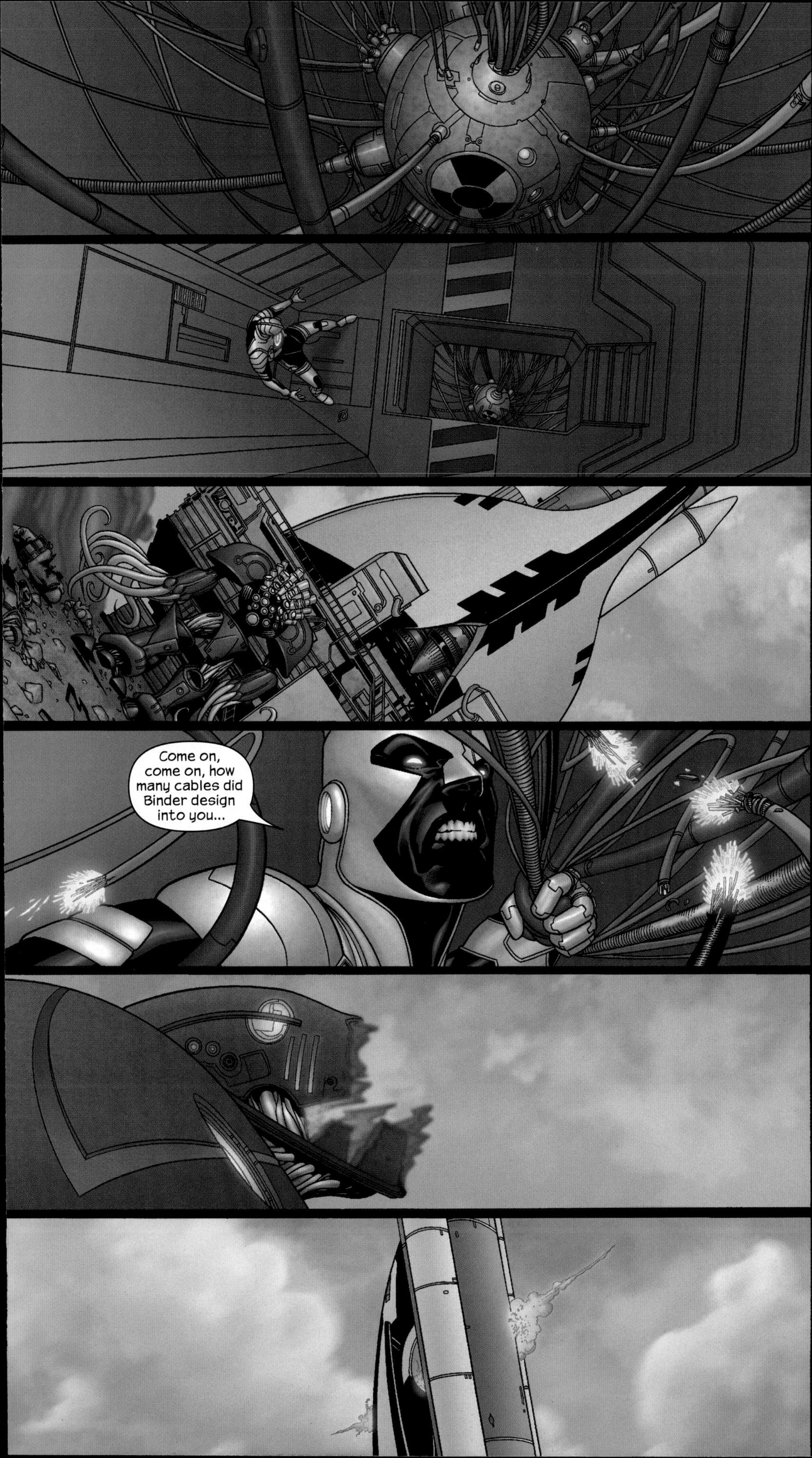
Come on, come on, how many cables did Binder design into you...

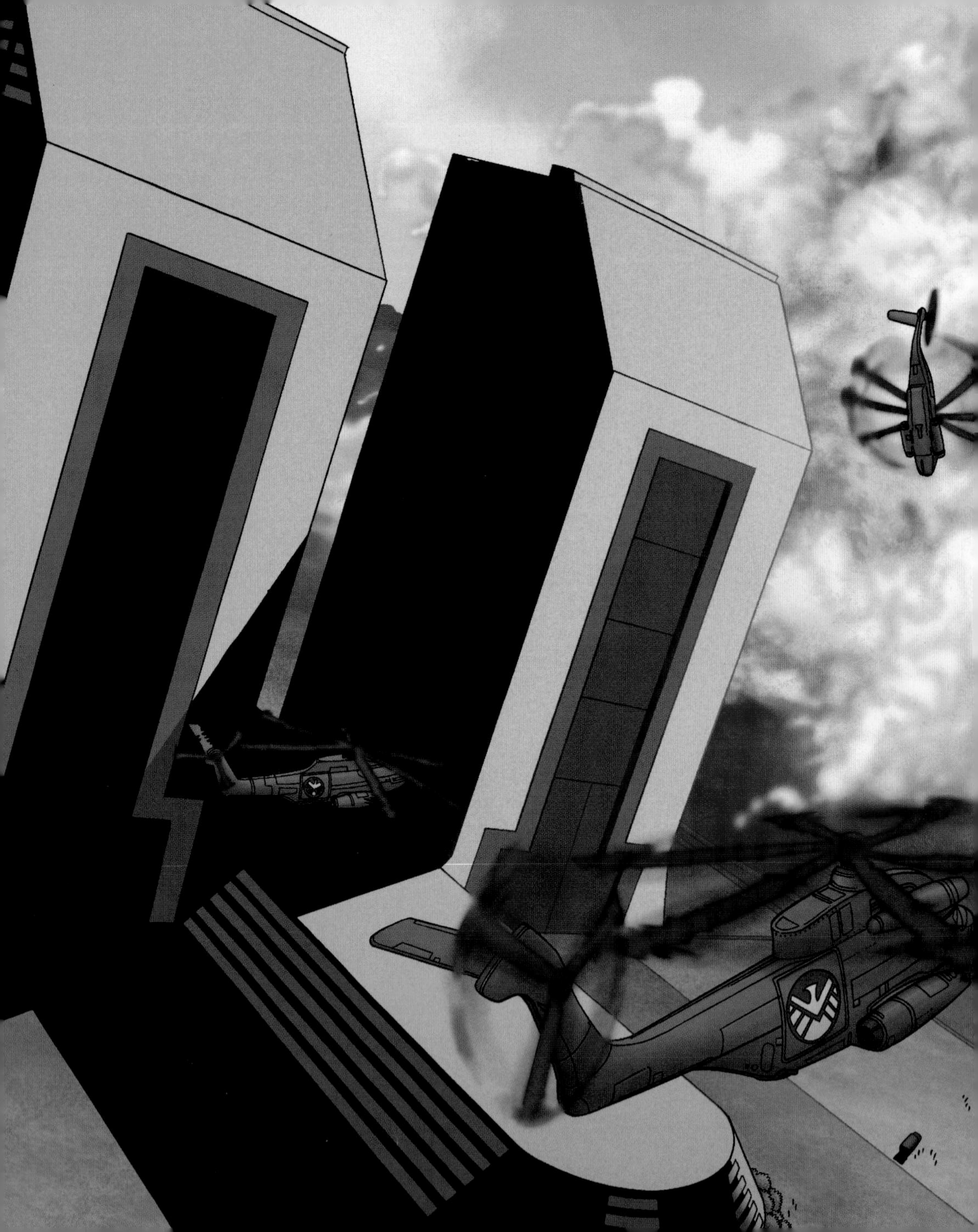

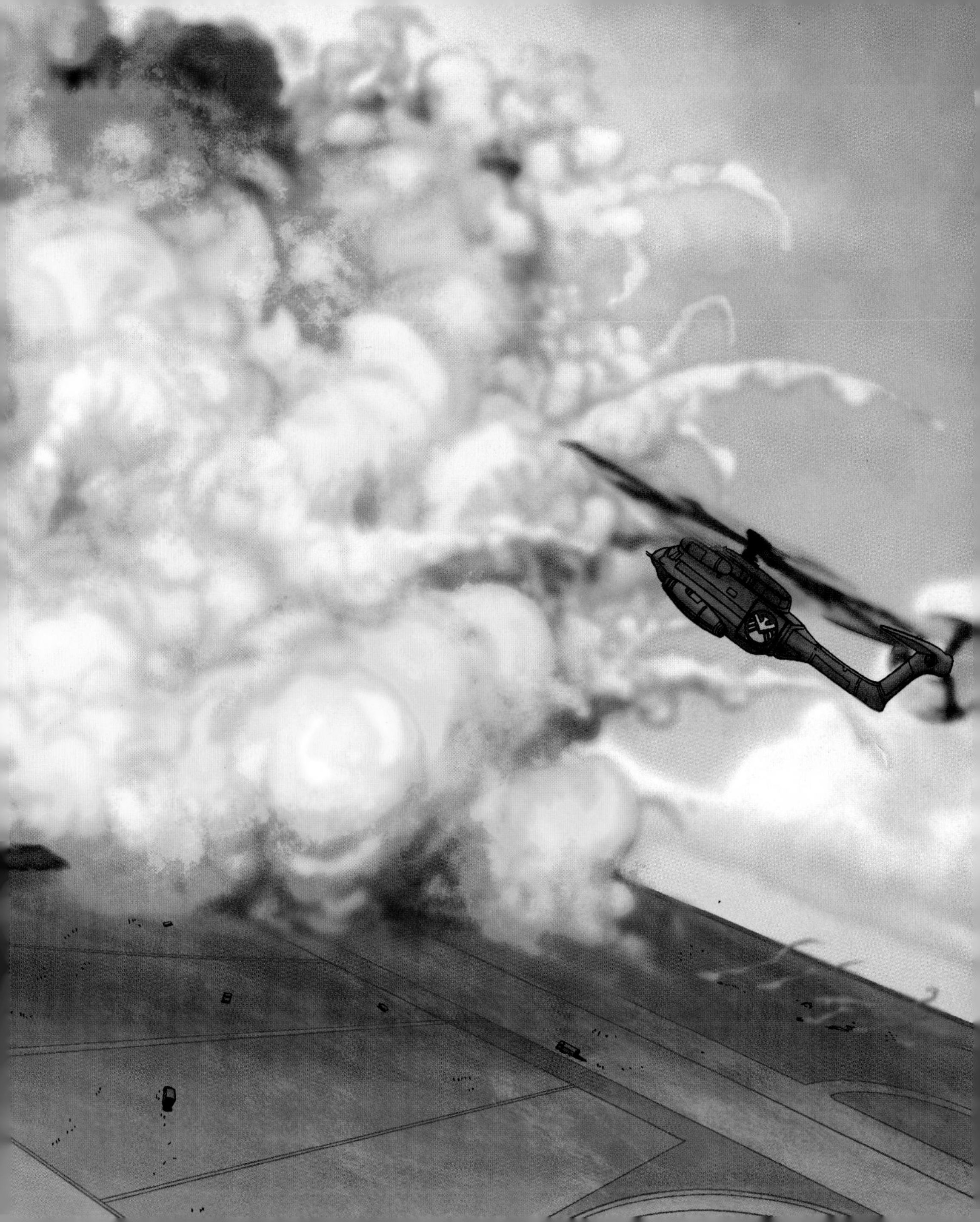

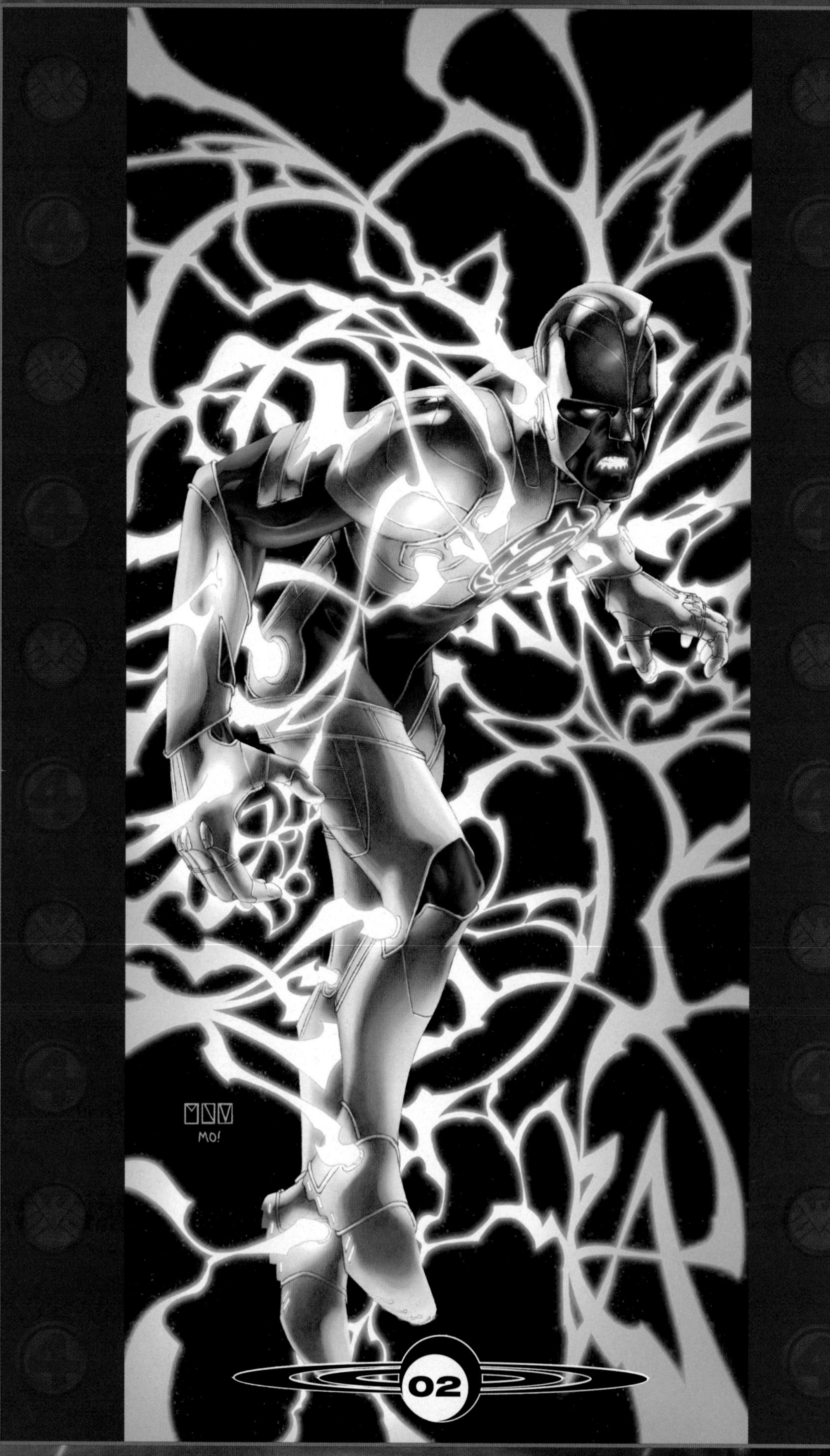
MO!
02

stan lee presents:

ULTIMATE SECRET

CHAPTER TWO

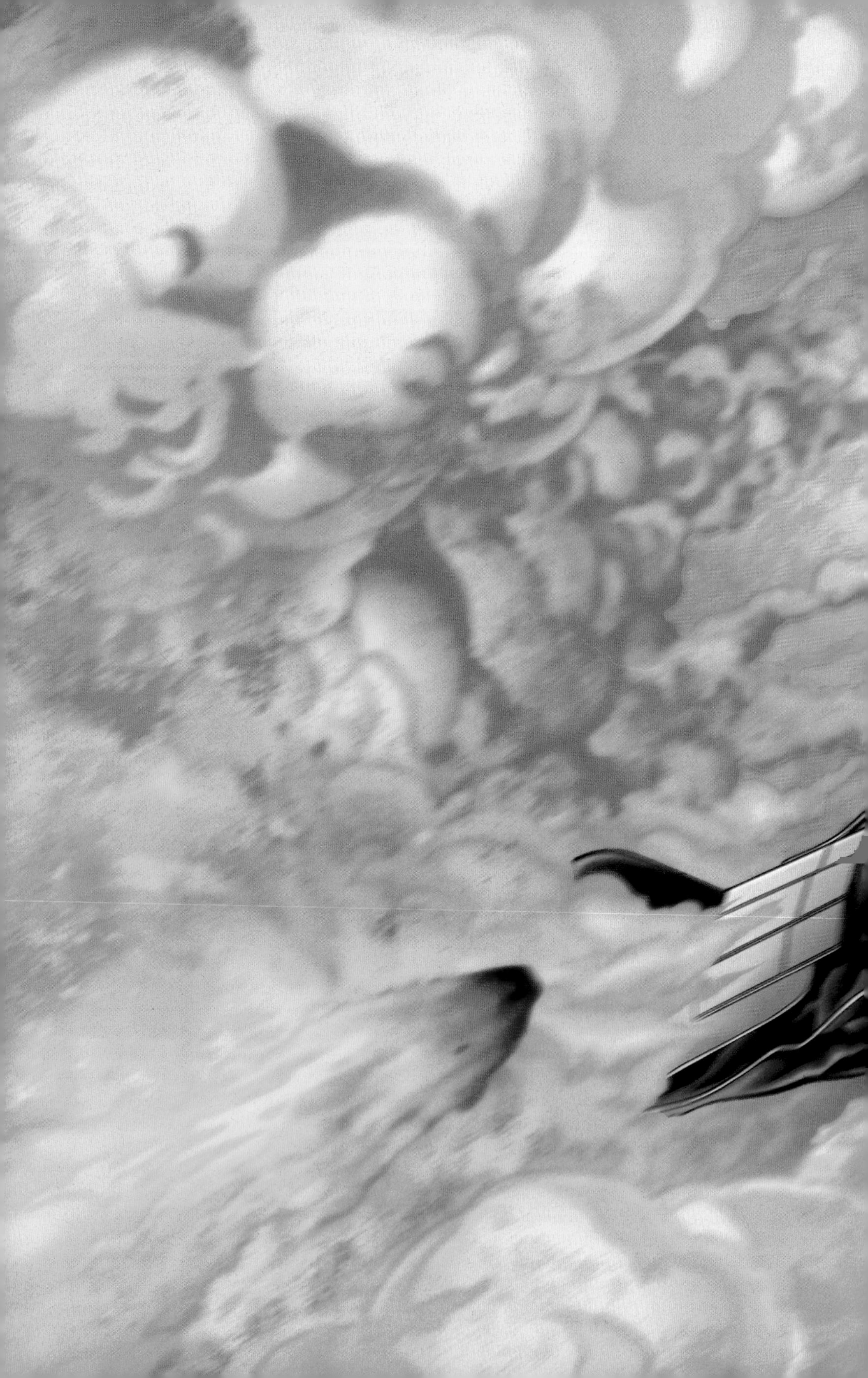

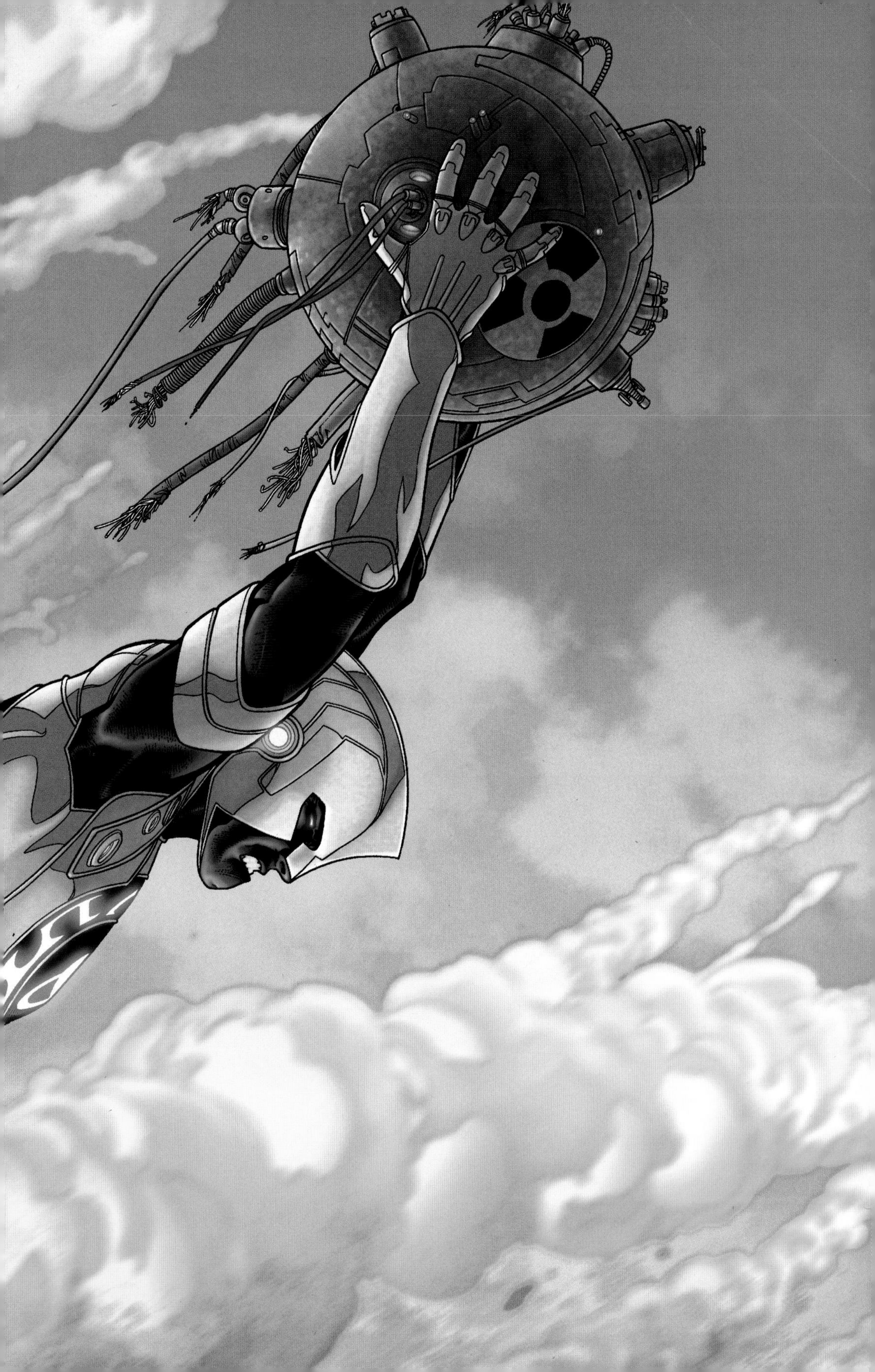

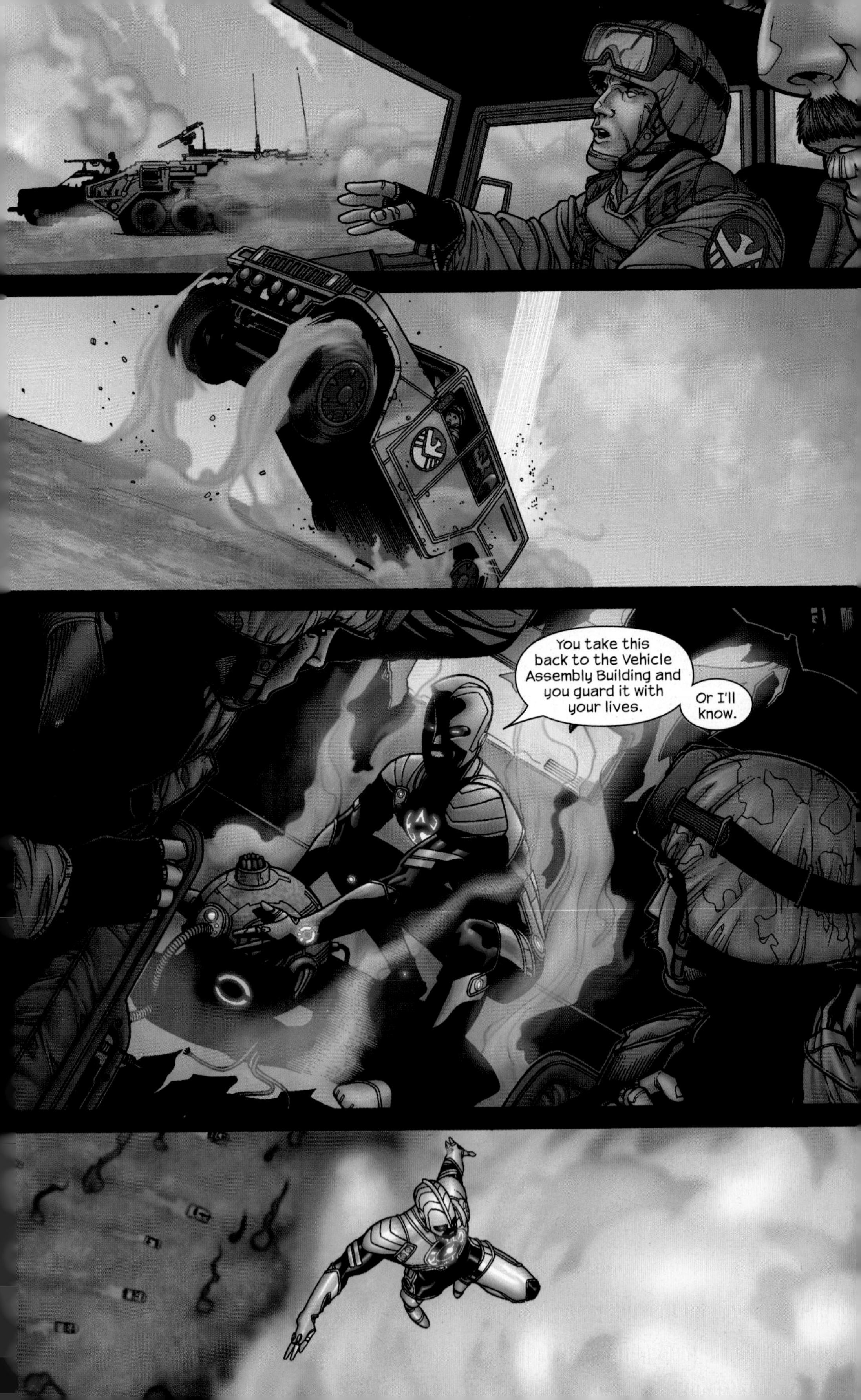
You take this back to the Vehicle Assembly Building and you guard it with your lives.
Or I'll know.

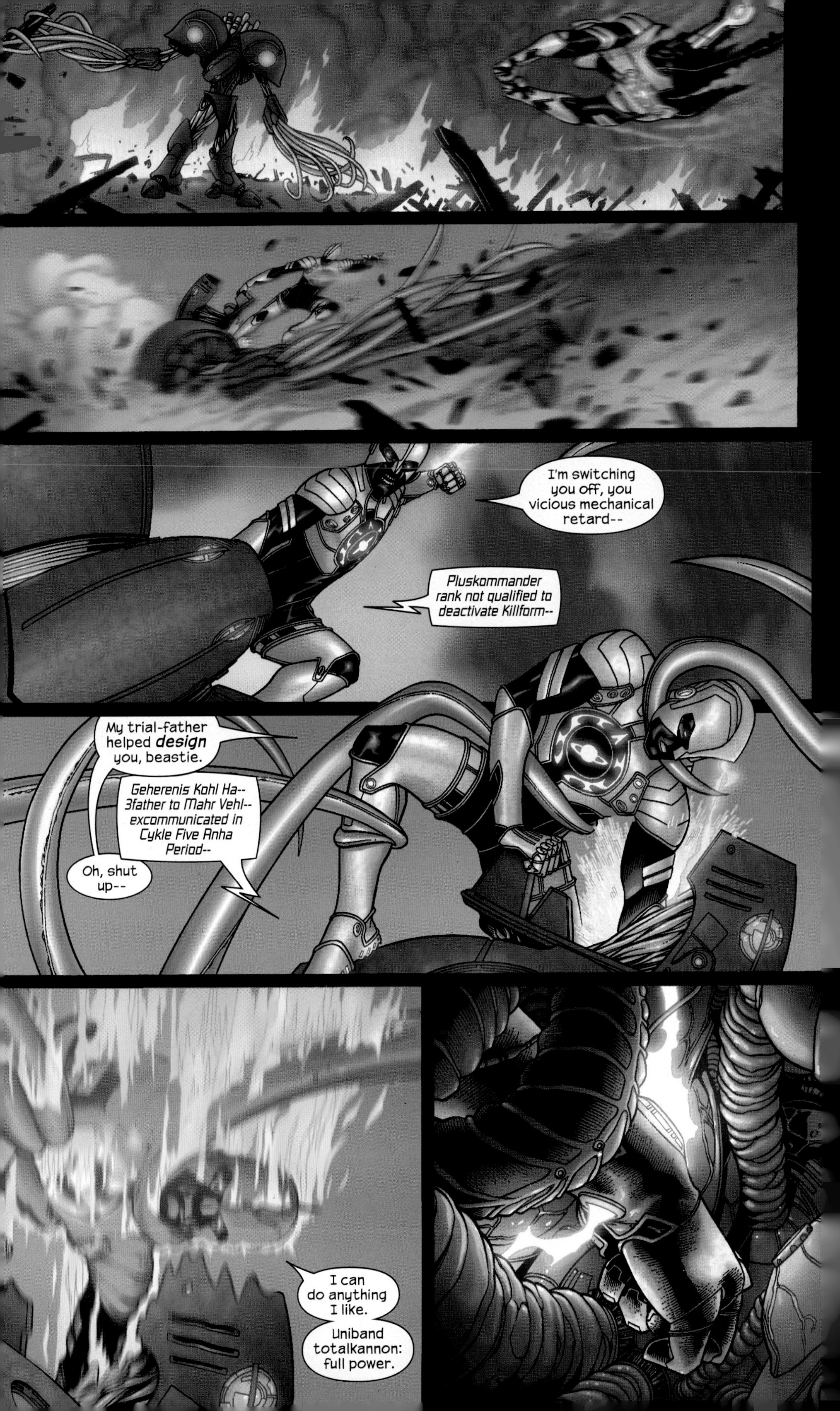

I'm switching you off, you vicious mechanical retard--
Pluskommander rank not qualified to deactivate Killform--
My trial-father helped *design* you, beastie.
Geherenis Kohl Ha--3father to Mahr Vehl--excommunicated in Cykle Five Anha Period--
Oh, shut up--
I can do anything I like.
Uniband totalkannon: full power.

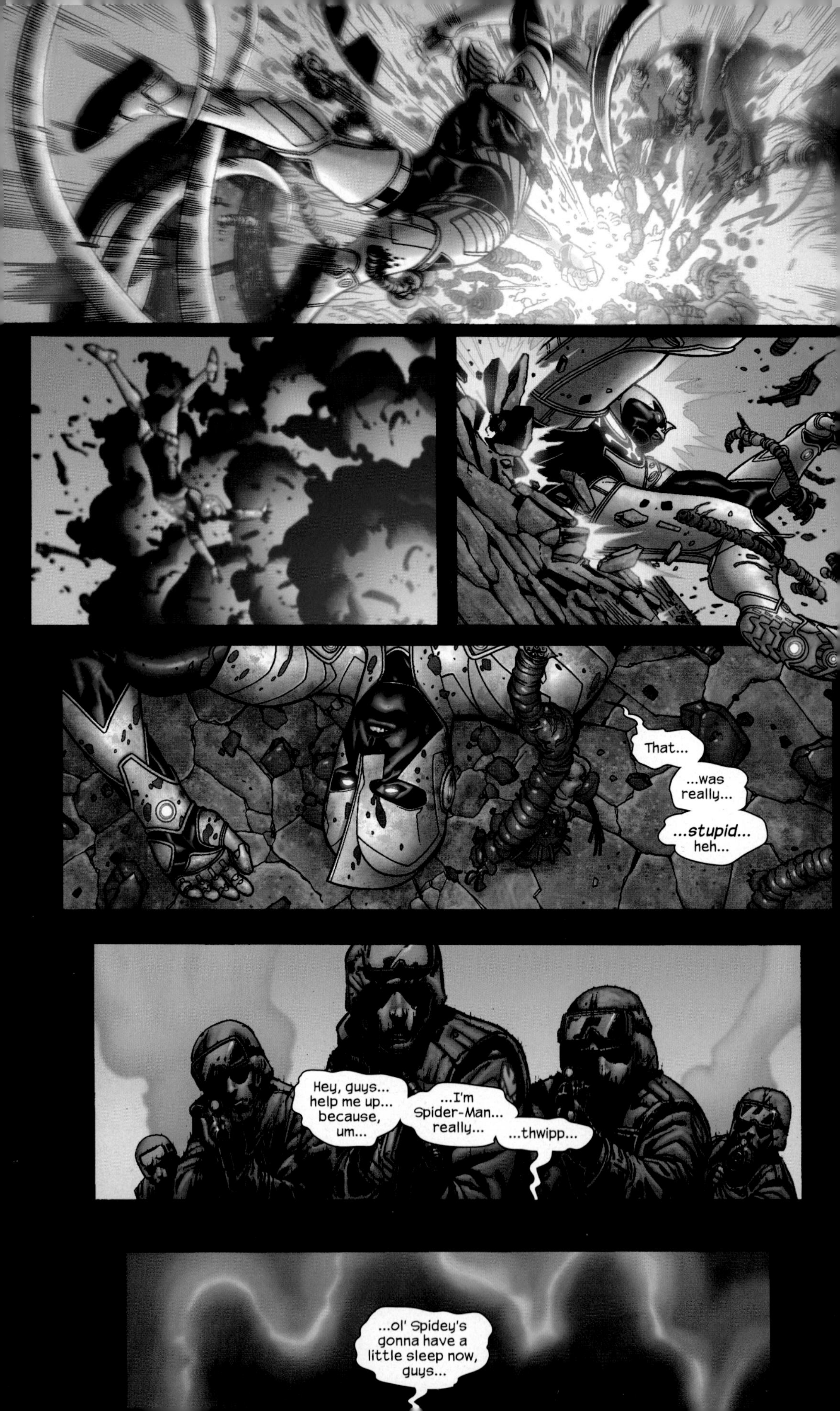
That...
...was really...
...stupid... heh...
Hey, guys... help me up... because, um...
...I'm Spider-Man... really...
...thwipp...
...ol' Spidey's gonna have a little sleep now, guys...

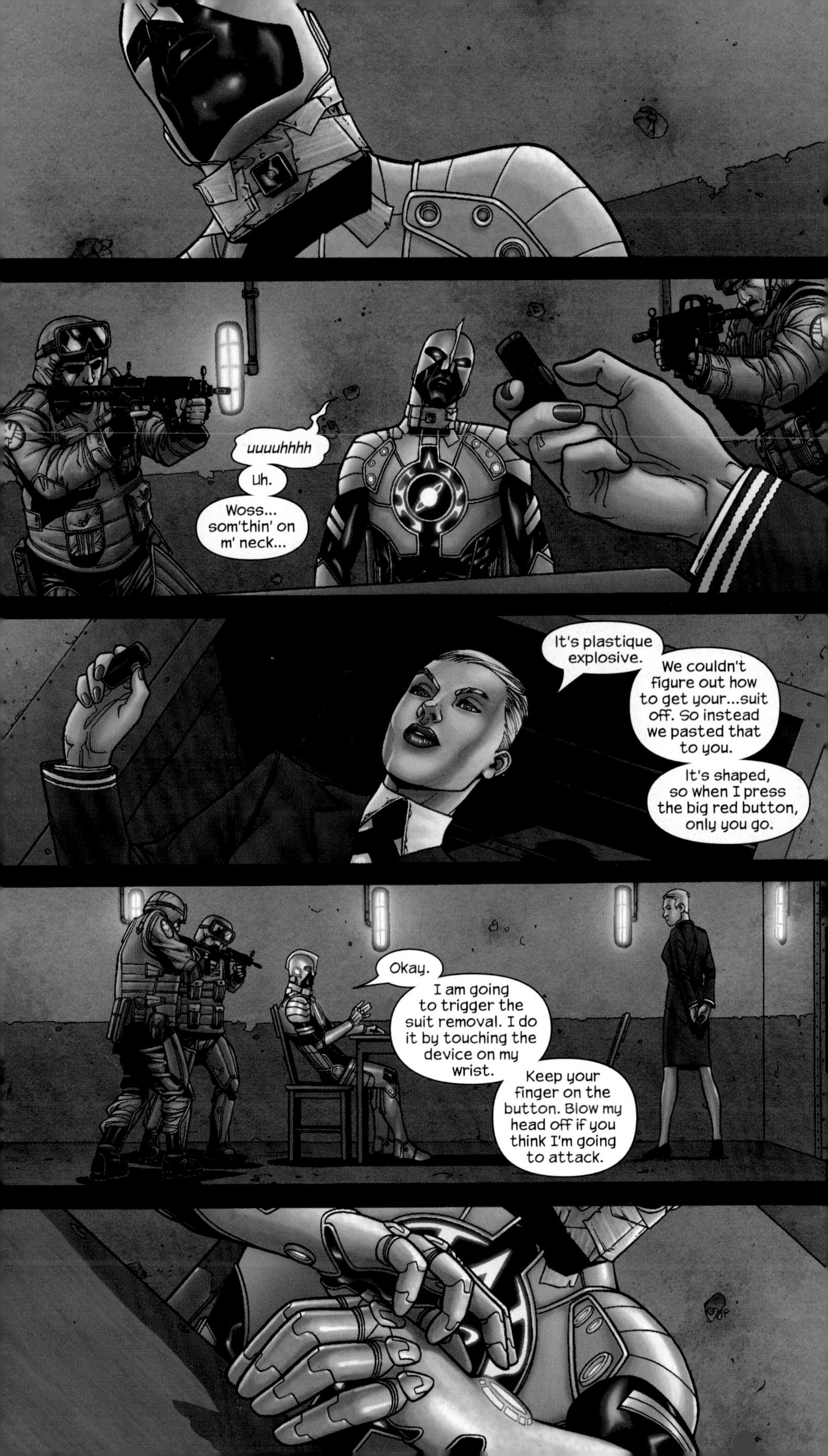
uuuuhhhh
Uh.
Woss... som'thin' on m' neck...
It's plastique explosive.
We couldn't figure out how to get your...suit off. So instead we pasted that to you.
It's shaped, so when I press the big red button, only you go.
Okay.
I am going to trigger the suit removal. I do it by touching the device on my wrist.
Keep your finger on the button. Blow my head off if you think I'm going to attack.

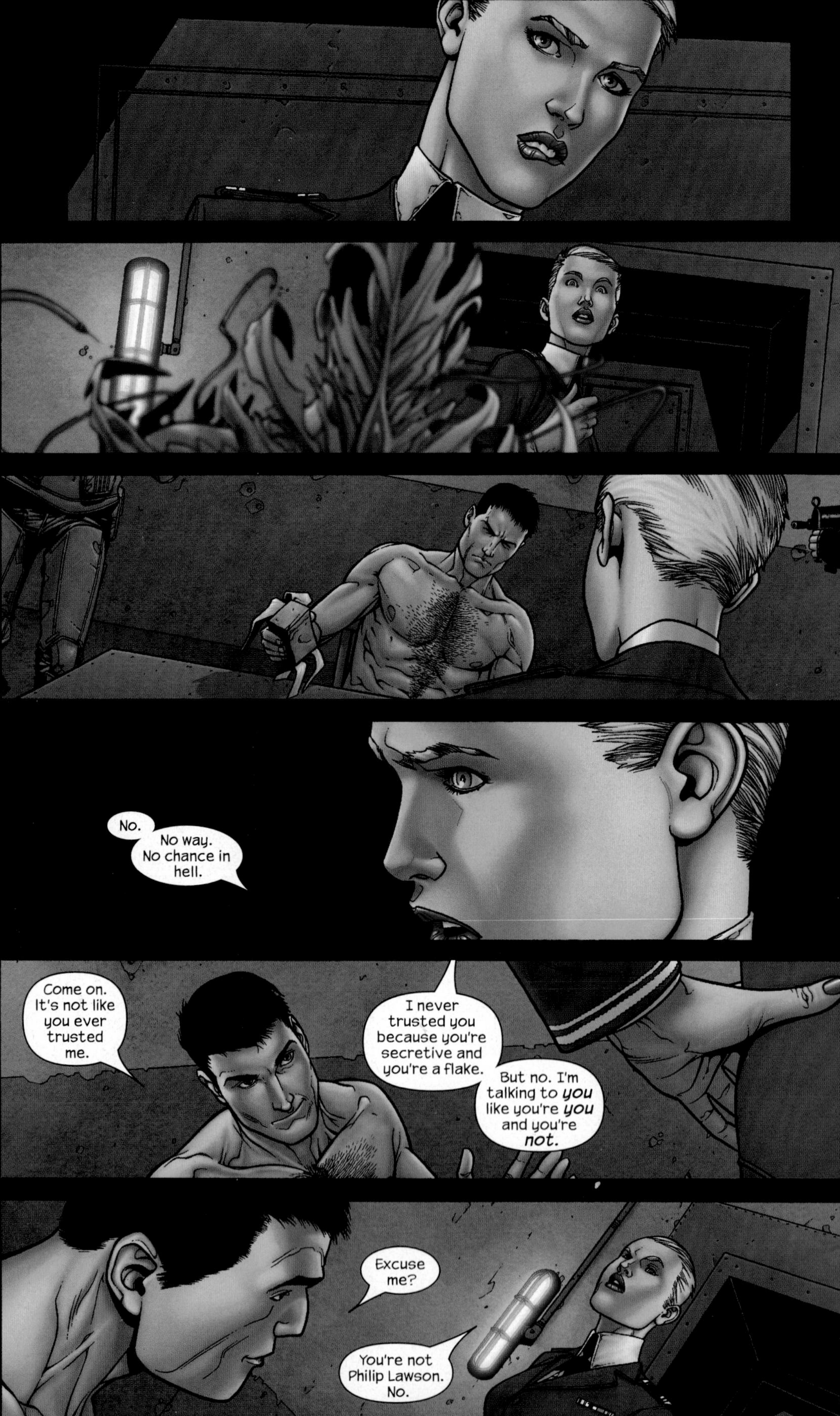
No.
No way. No chance in hell.
Come on. It's not like you ever trusted me.
I never trusted you because you're secretive and you're a flake.
But no. I'm talking to *you* like you're *you* and you're ***not.***
Excuse me?
You're not Philip Lawson. No.

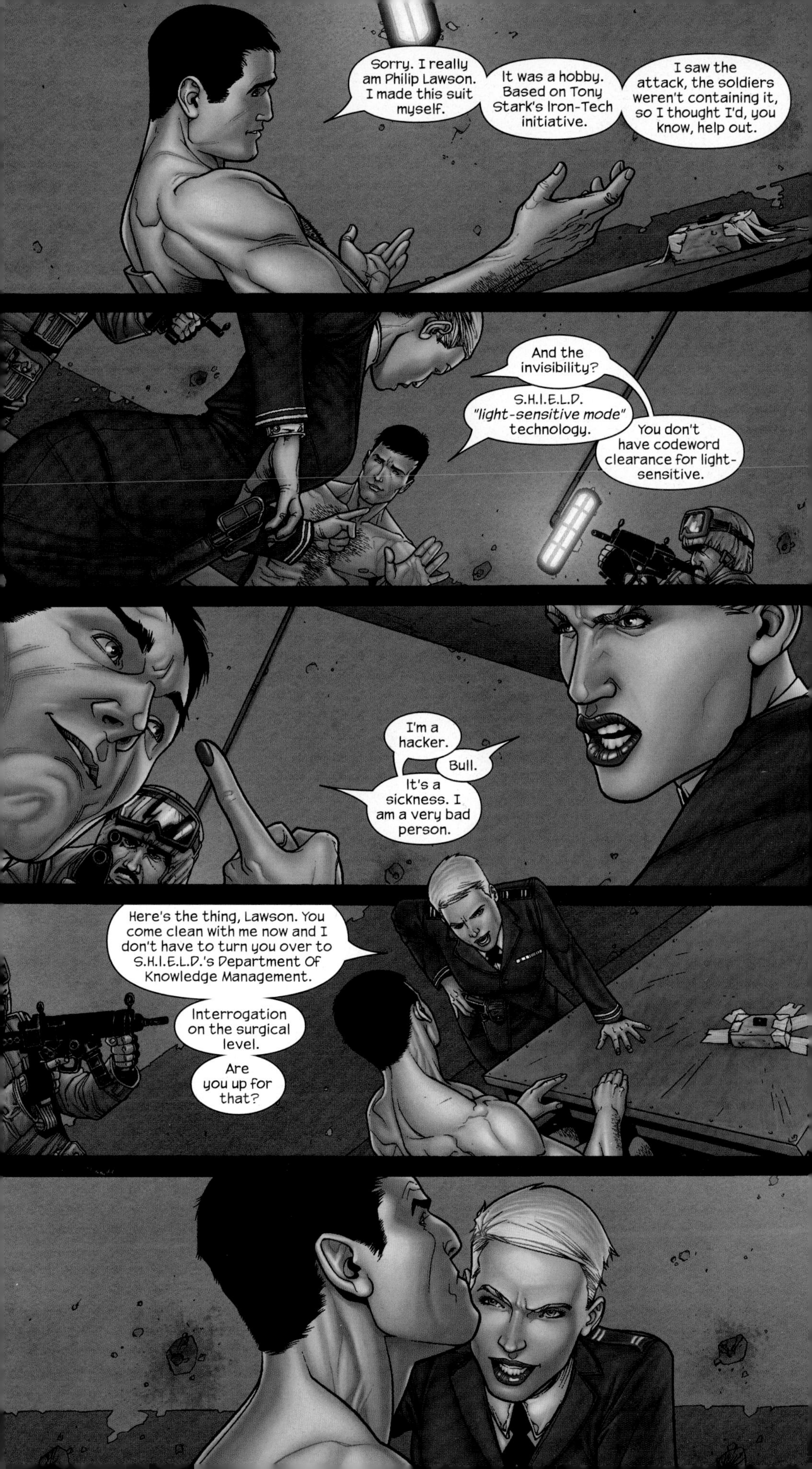

Sorry. I really am Philip Lawson. I made this suit myself.
It was a hobby. Based on Tony Stark's Iron-Tech initiative.
I saw the attack, the soldiers weren't containing it, so I thought I'd, you know, help out.
And the invisibility?
S.H.I.E.L.D. "light-sensitive mode" technology.
You don't have codeword clearance for light-sensitive.
I'm a hacker.
Bull.
It's a sickness. I am a very bad person.
Here's the thing, Lawson. You come clean with me now and I don't have to turn you over to S.H.I.E.L.D.'s Department Of Knowledge Management.
Interrogation on the surgical level.
Are you up for that?

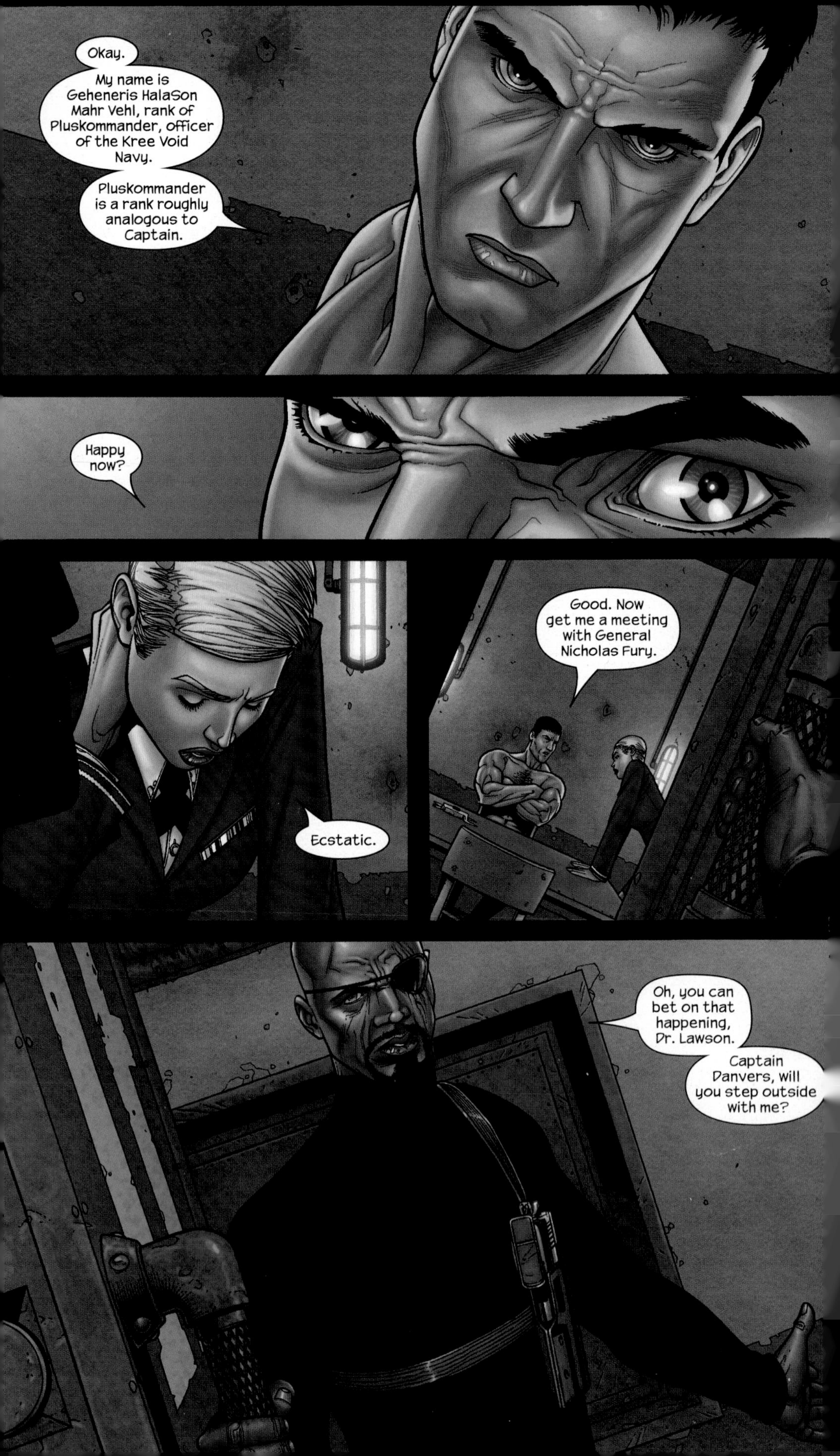
Okay.
My name is Geheneris HalaSon Mahr Vehl, rank of Pluskommander, officer of the Kree Void Navy.
Pluskommander is a rank roughly analogous to Captain.
Happy now?
Ecstatic.
Good. Now get me a meeting with General Nicholas Fury.
Oh, you can bet on that happening, Dr. Lawson.
Captain Danvers, will you step outside with me?

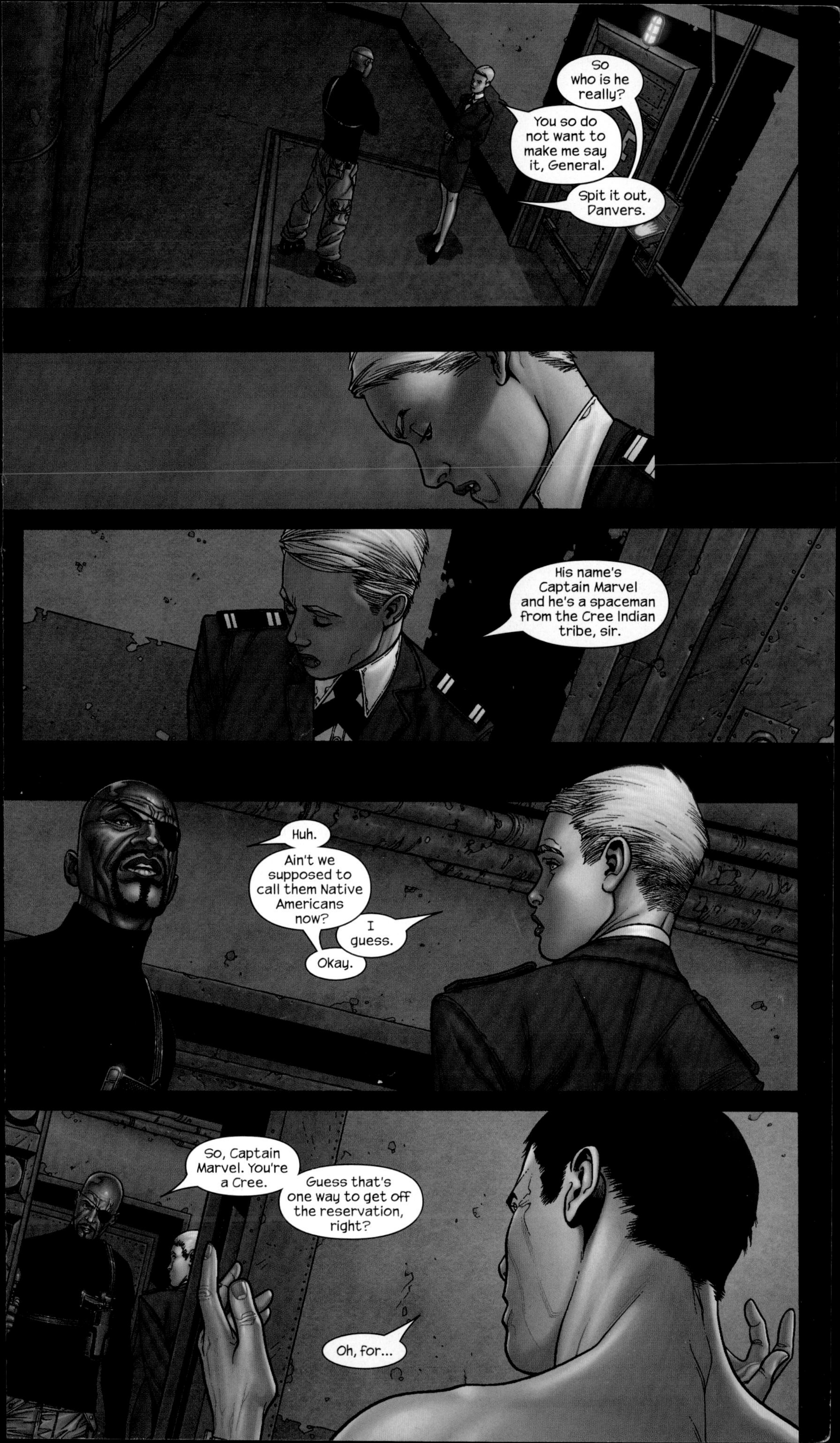
So who is he really?
You so do not want to make me say it, General.
Spit it out, Danvers.
His name's Captain Marvel and he's a spaceman from the Cree Indian tribe, sir.
Huh.
Ain't we supposed to call them Native Americans now?
I guess.
Okay.
So, Captain Marvel. You're a Cree.
Guess that's one way to get off the reservation, right?
Oh, for...

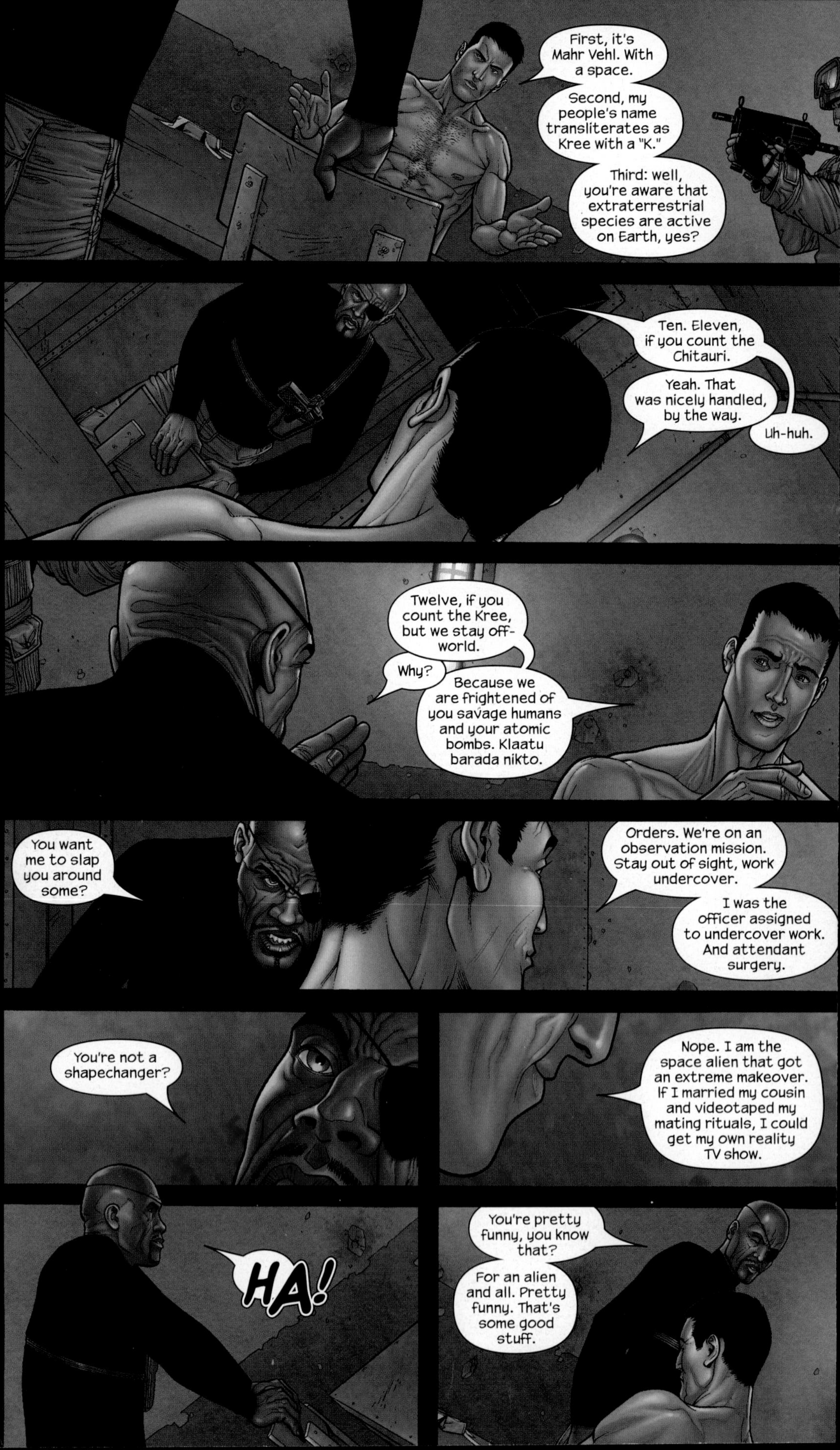
First, it's Mahr Vehl. With a space.
Second, my people's name transliterates as Kree with a "K."
Third: well, you're aware that extraterrestrial species are active on Earth, yes?
Ten. Eleven, if you count the Chitauri.
Yeah. That was nicely handled, by the way.
Uh-huh.
Twelve, if you count the Kree, but we stay off-world.
Why?
Because we are frightened of you savage humans and your atomic bombs. Klaatu barada nikto.
You want me to slap you around some?
Orders. We're on an observation mission. Stay out of sight, work undercover.
I was the officer assigned to undercover work. And attendant surgery.
You're not a shapechanger?
Nope. I am the space alien that got an extreme makeover. If I married my cousin and videotaped my mating rituals, I could get my own reality TV show.
HA!
You're pretty funny, you know that?
For an alien and all. Pretty funny. That's some good stuff.

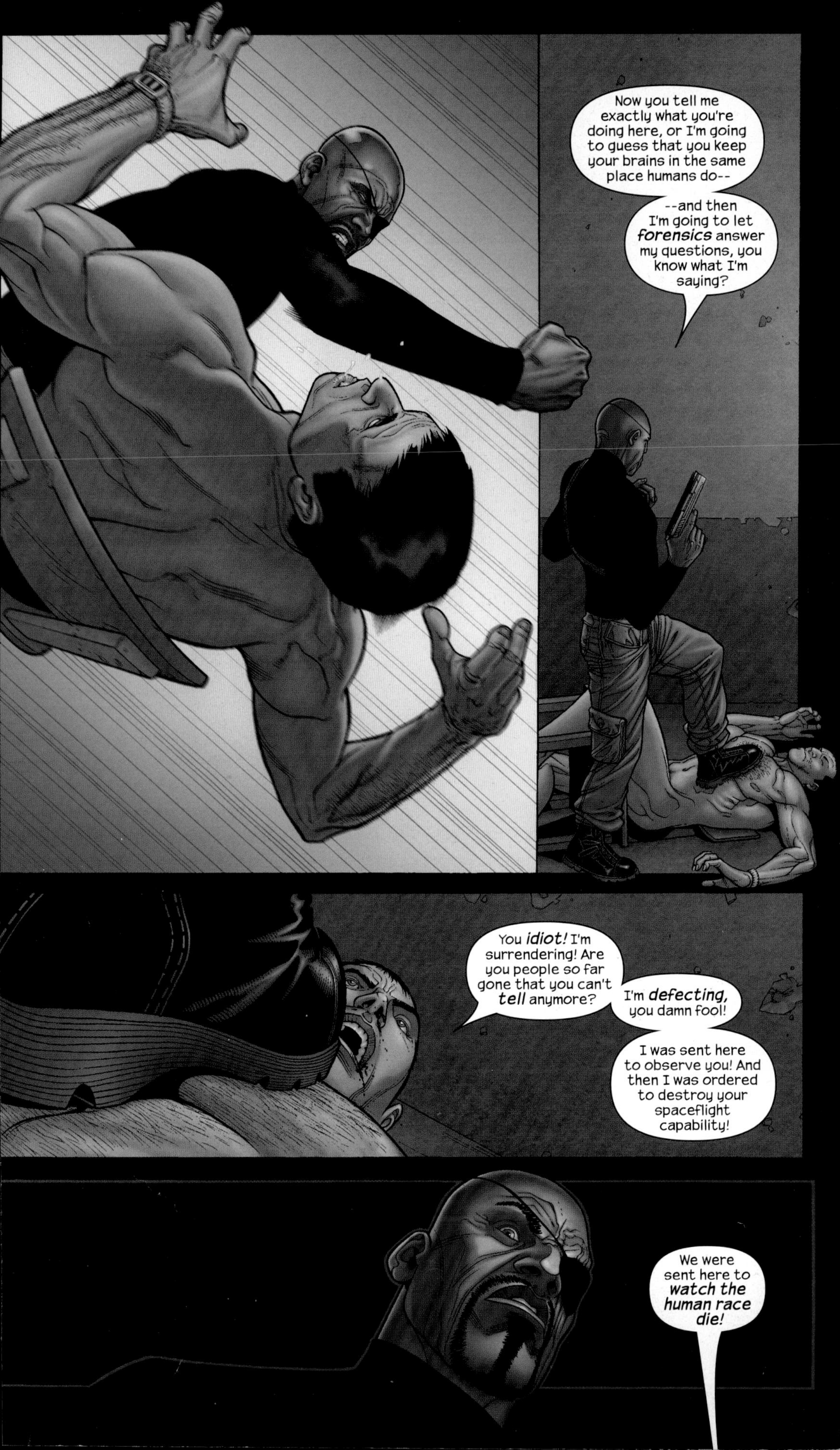
Now you tell me exactly what you're doing here, or I'm going to guess that you keep your brains in the same place humans do--
--and then I'm going to let *forensics* answer my questions, you know what I'm saying?
You *idiot!* I'm surrendering! Are you people so far gone that you can't *tell* anymore?
I'm *defecting,* you damn fool!
I was sent here to observe you! And then I was ordered to destroy your spaceflight capability!
We were sent here to ***watch the human race die!***

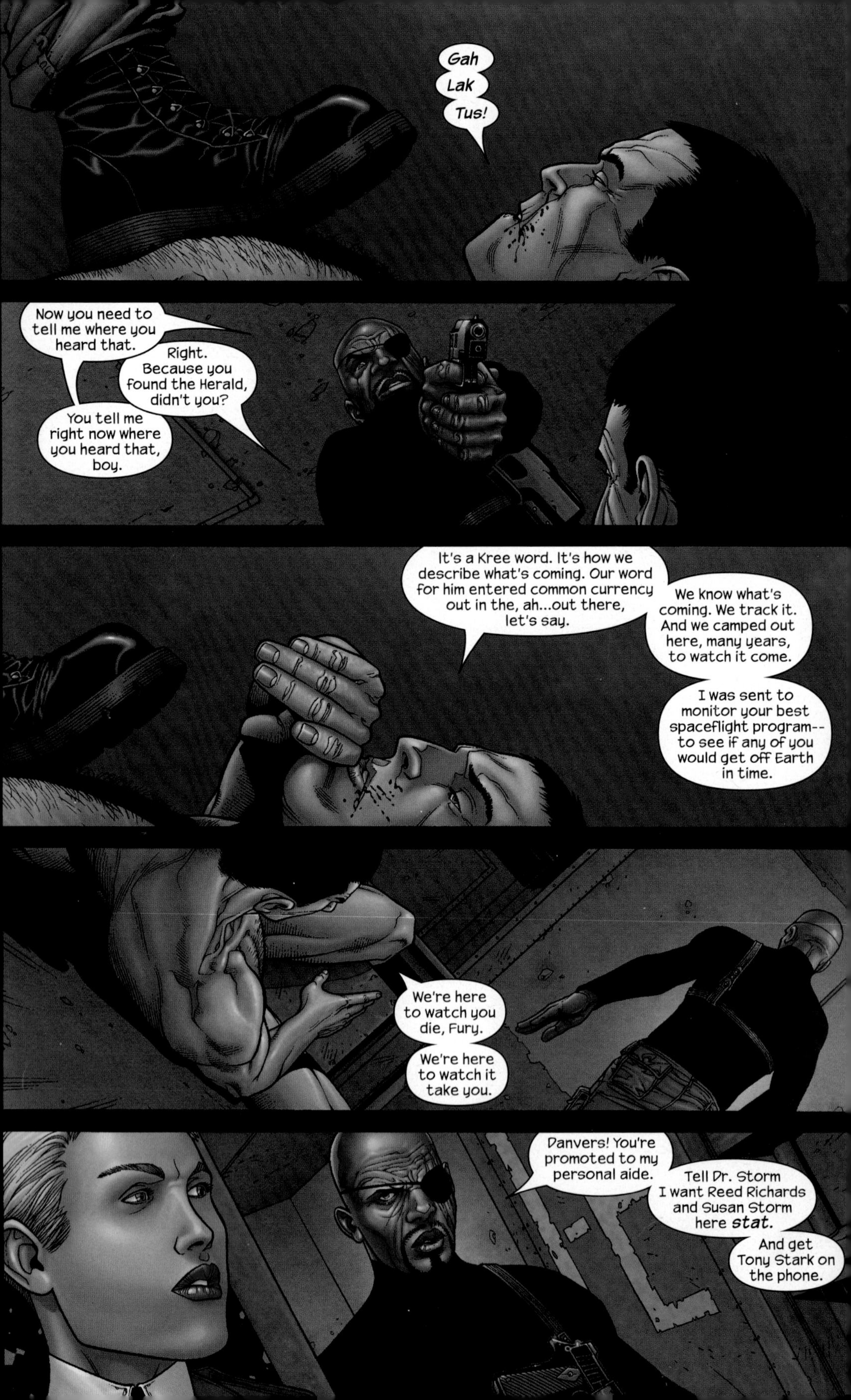
Gah
Lak
Tus!
Now you need to tell me where you heard that.
Right. Because you found the Herald, didn't you?
You tell me right now where you heard that, boy.
It's a Kree word. It's how we describe what's coming. Our word for him entered common currency out in the, ah...out there, let's say.
We know what's coming. We track it. And we camped out here, many years, to watch it come.
I was sent to monitor your best spaceflight program--to see if any of you would get off Earth in time.
We're here to watch you die, Fury.
We're here to watch it take you.
Danvers! You're promoted to my personal aide.
Tell Dr. Storm I want Reed Richards and Susan Storm here stat.
And get Tony Stark on the phone.

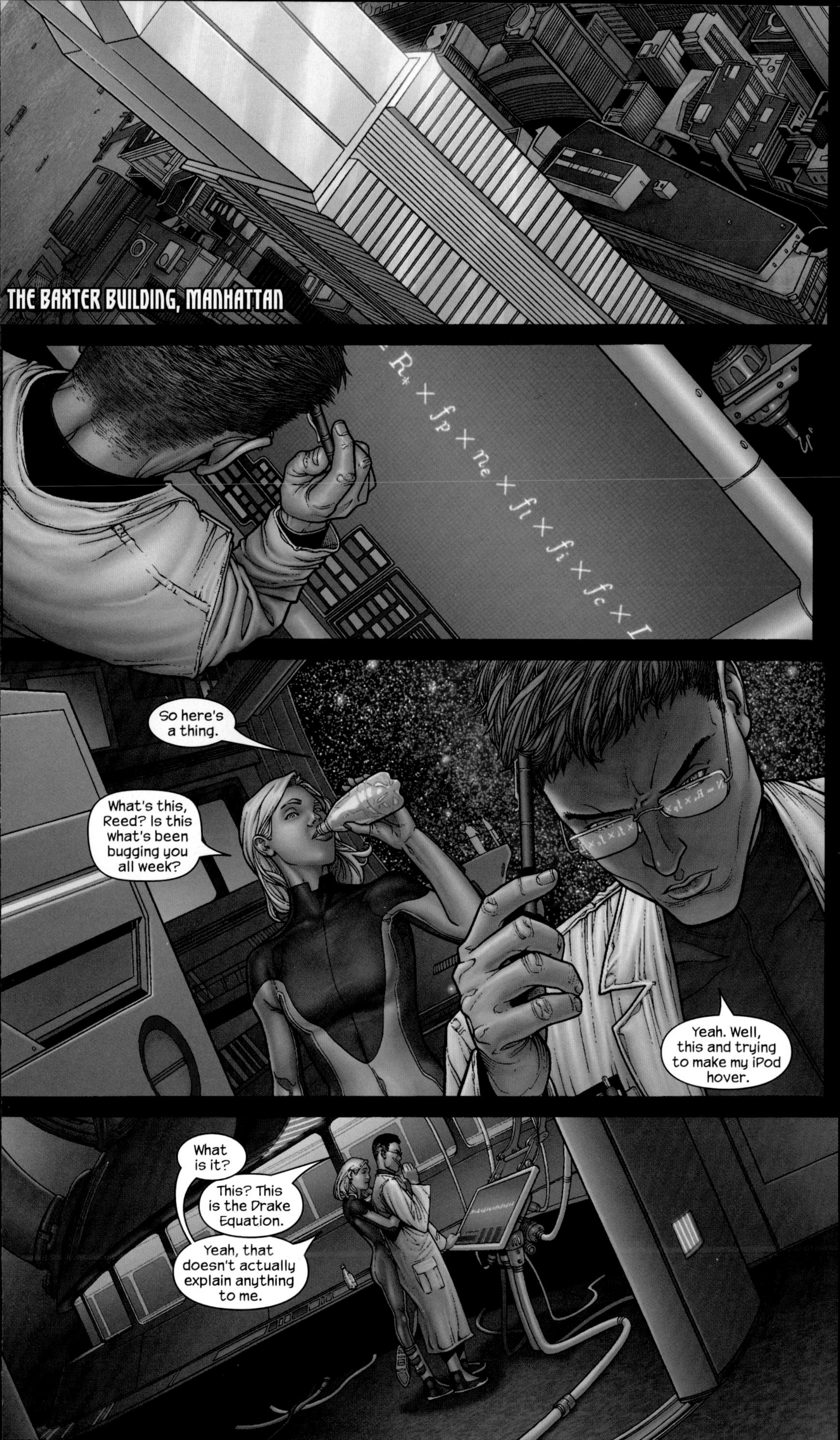
THE BAXTER BUILDING, MANHATTAN
So here's a thing.
What's this, Reed? Is this what's been bugging you all week?
Yeah. Well, this and trying to make my iPod hover.
What is it?
This? This is the Drake Equation.
Yeah, that doesn't actually explain anything to me.

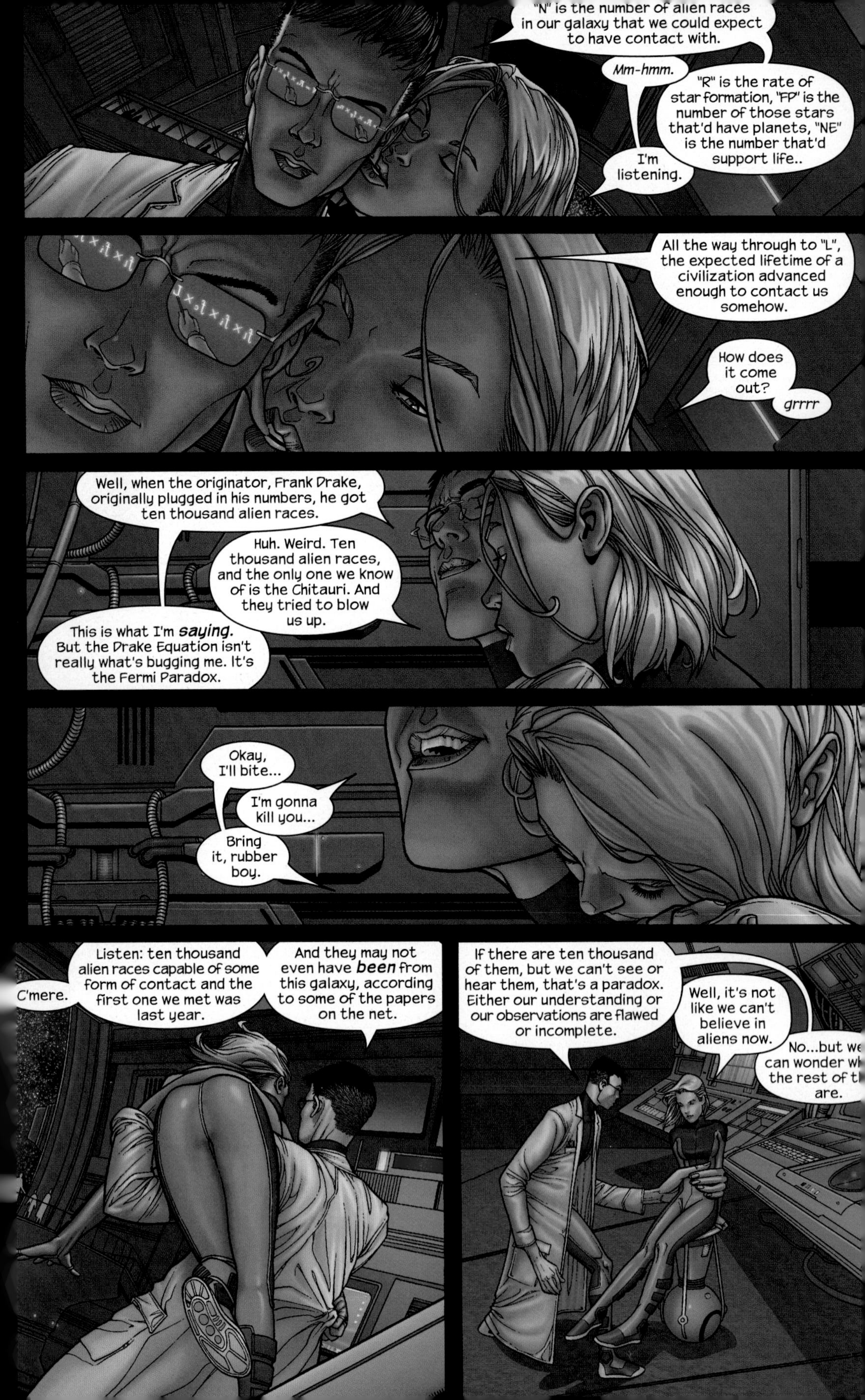
"N" is the number of alien races in our galaxy that we could expect to have contact with.
Mm-hmm.
"R" is the rate of star formation, "FP" is the number of those stars that'd have planets, "NE" is the number that'd support life..
I'm listening.
All the way through to "L", the expected lifetime of a civilization advanced enough to contact us somehow.
How does it come out?
grrrr
Well, when the originator, Frank Drake, originally plugged in his numbers, he got ten thousand alien races.
Huh. Weird. Ten thousand alien races, and the only one we know of is the Chitauri. And they tried to blow us up.
This is what I'm saying. But the Drake Equation isn't really what's bugging me. It's the Fermi Paradox.
Okay, I'll bite...
I'm gonna kill you...
Bring it, rubber boy.
C'mere.
Listen: ten thousand alien races capable of some form of contact and the first one we met was last year.
And they may not even have been from this galaxy, according to some of the papers on the net.
If there are ten thousand of them, but we can't see or hear them, that's a paradox. Either our understanding or our observations are flawed or incomplete.
Well, it's not like we can't believe in aliens now.

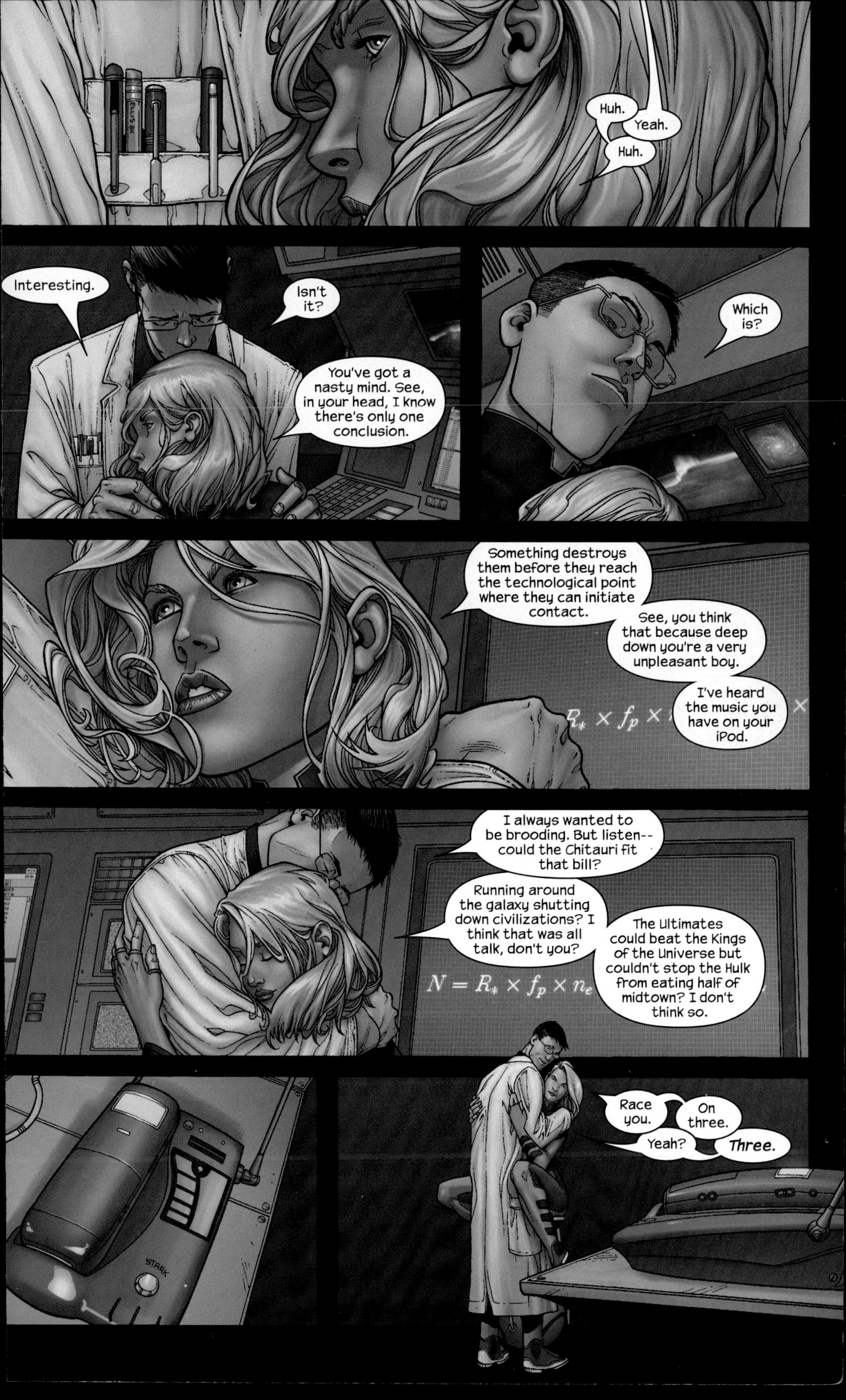
Huh.
Yeah.
Huh.
Interesting.
Isn't it?
You've got a nasty mind. See, in your head, I know there's only one conclusion.
Which is?
Something destroys them before they reach the technological point where they can initiate contact.
See, you think that because deep down you're a very unpleasant boy.
I've heard the music you have on your iPod.
I always wanted to be brooding. But listen-- could the Chitauri fit that bill?
Running around the galaxy shutting down civilizations? I think that was all talk, don't you?
The Ultimates could beat the Kings of the Universe but couldn't stop the Hulk from eating half of midtown? I don't think so.
STARK
Race you.
On three.
Yeah?
Three.

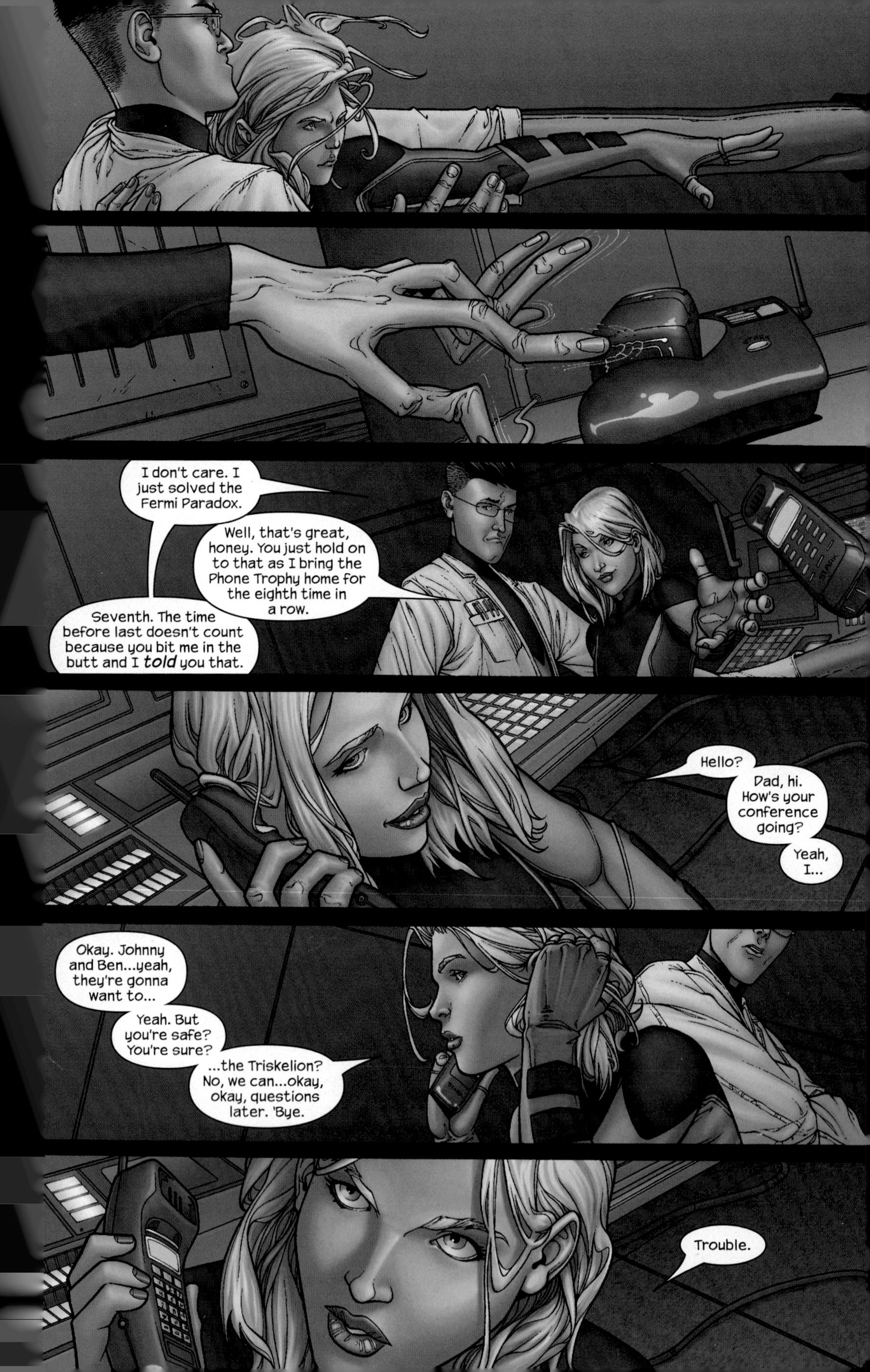
I don't care. I just solved the Fermi Paradox.
Well, that's great, honey. You just hold on to that as I bring the Phone Trophy home for the eighth time in a row.
Seventh. The time before last doesn't count because you bit me in the butt and I *told* you that.
Hello?
Dad, hi. How's your conference going?
Yeah, I...
Okay. Johnny and Ben...yeah, they're gonna want to...
Yeah. But you're safe? You're sure?
...the Triskelion? No, we can...okay, okay, questions later. 'Bye.
Trouble.

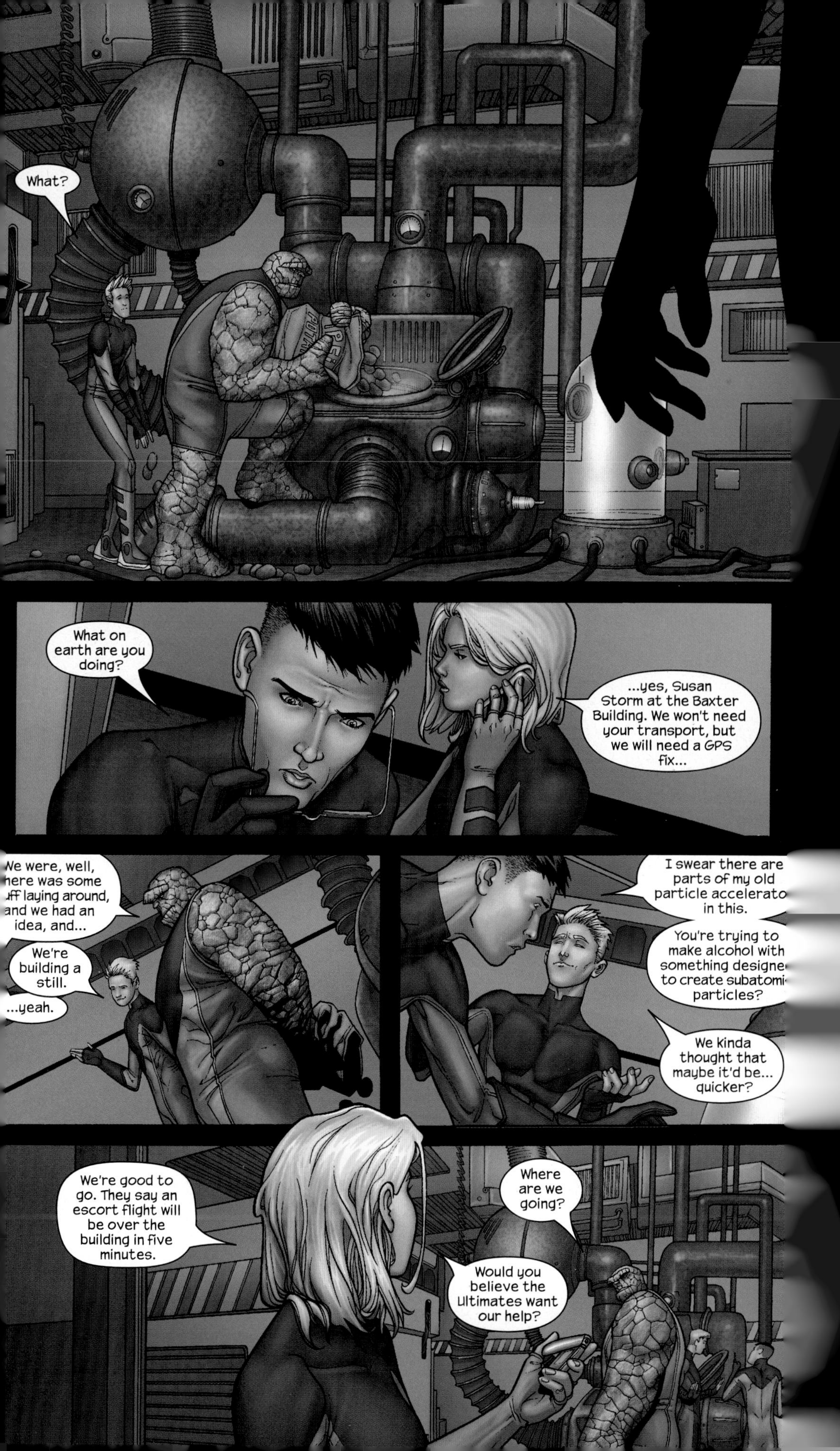
What?
What on earth are you doing?
...yes, Susan Storm at the Baxter Building. We won't need your transport, but we will need a GPS fix...
We were, well, here was some uff laying around, and we had an idea, and...
We're building a still.
...yeah.
I swear there are parts of my old particle accelerato in this.
You're trying to make alcohol with something designe to create subatomi particles?
We kinda thought that maybe it'd be... quicker?
We're good to go. They say an escort flight will be over the building in five minutes.
Where are we going?
Would you believe the Ultimates want our help?

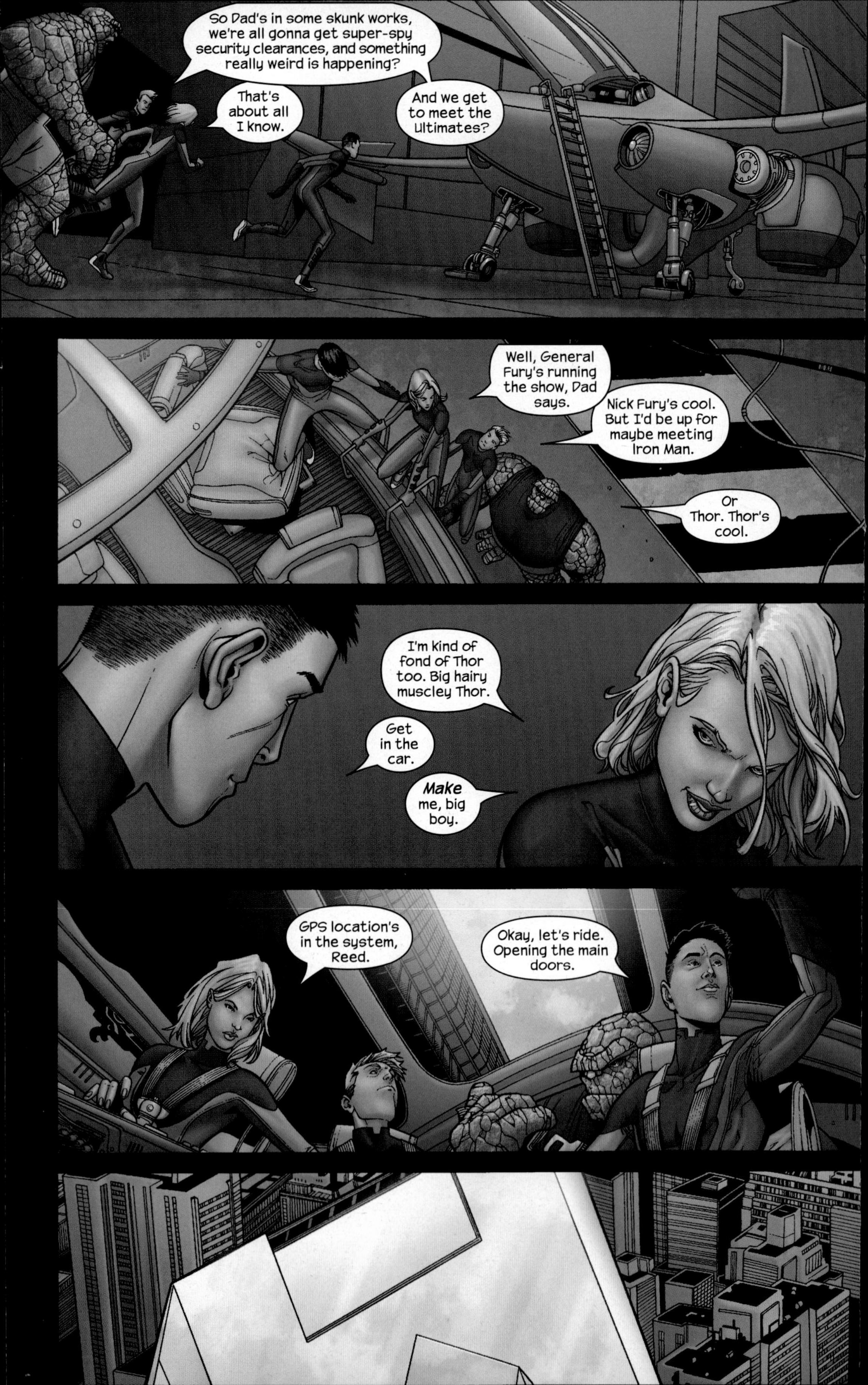
So Dad's in some skunk works, we're all gonna get super-spy security clearances, and something really weird is happening?
That's about all I know.
And we get to meet the Ultimates?
Well, General Fury's running the show, Dad says.
Nick Fury's cool. But I'd be up for maybe meeting Iron Man.
Or Thor. Thor's cool.
I'm kind of fond of Thor too. Big hairy muscley Thor.
Get in the car.
Make me, big boy.
GPS location's in the system, Reed.
Okay, let's ride. Opening the main doors.

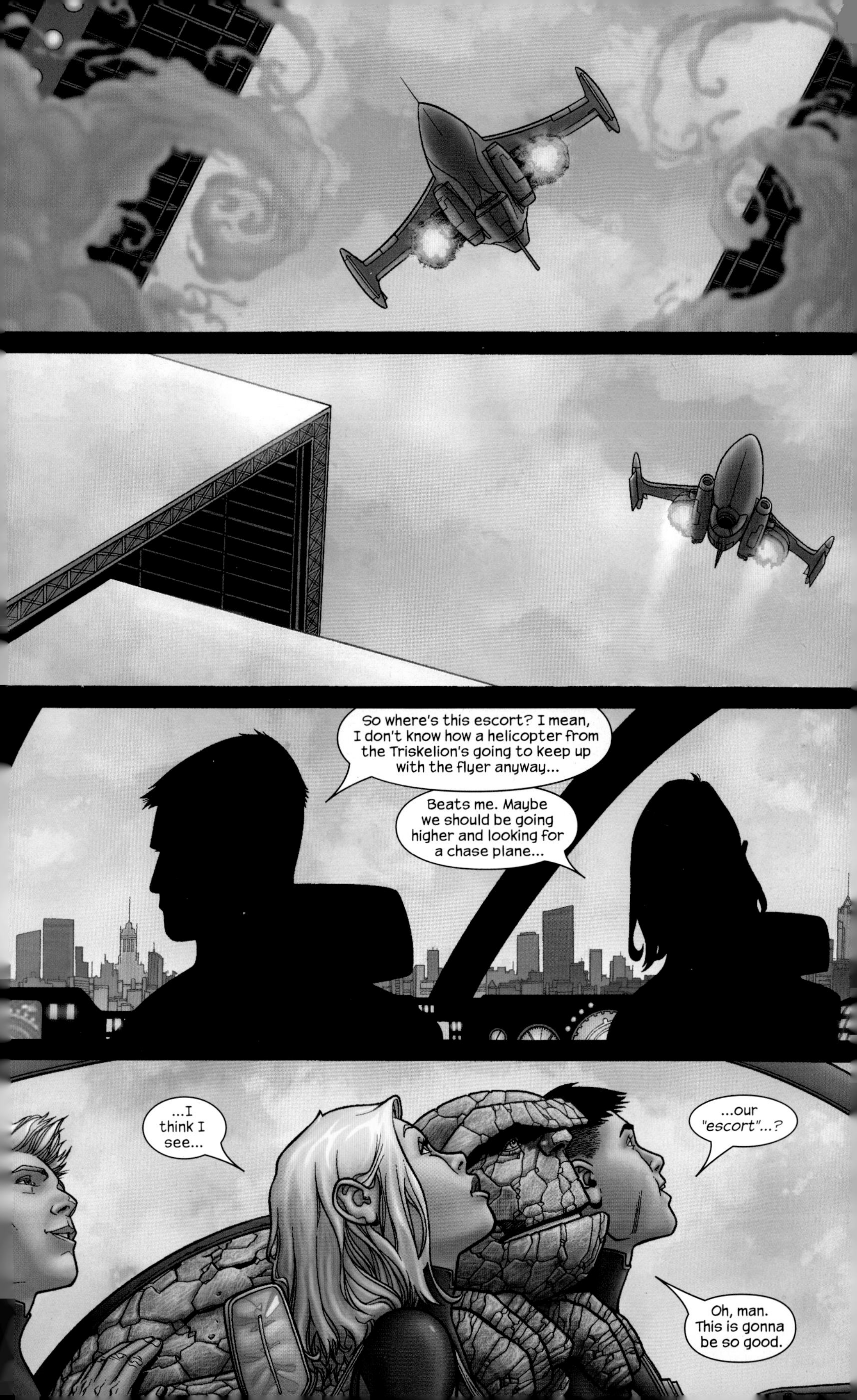
So where's this escort? I mean, I don't know how a helicopter from the Triskelion's going to keep up with the flyer anyway...
Beats me. Maybe we should be going higher and looking for a chase plane...
...I think I see...
...our "escort"...?
Oh, man. This is gonna be so good.

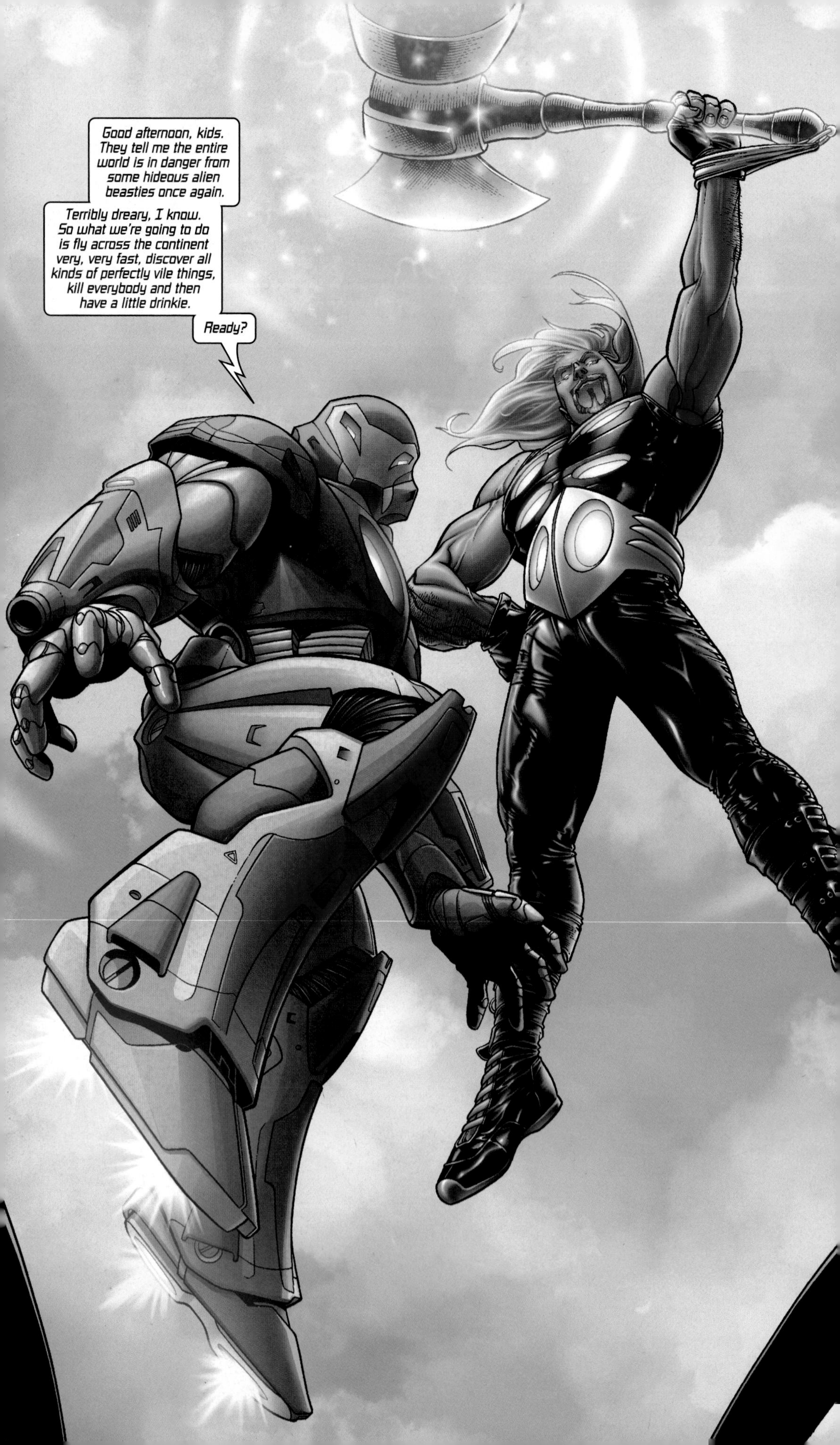
Good afternoon, kids. They tell me the entire world is in danger from some hideous alien beasties once again.
Terribly dreary, I know. So what we're going to do is fly across the continent very, very fast, discover all kinds of perfectly vile things, kill everybody and then have a little drinkie.
Ready?

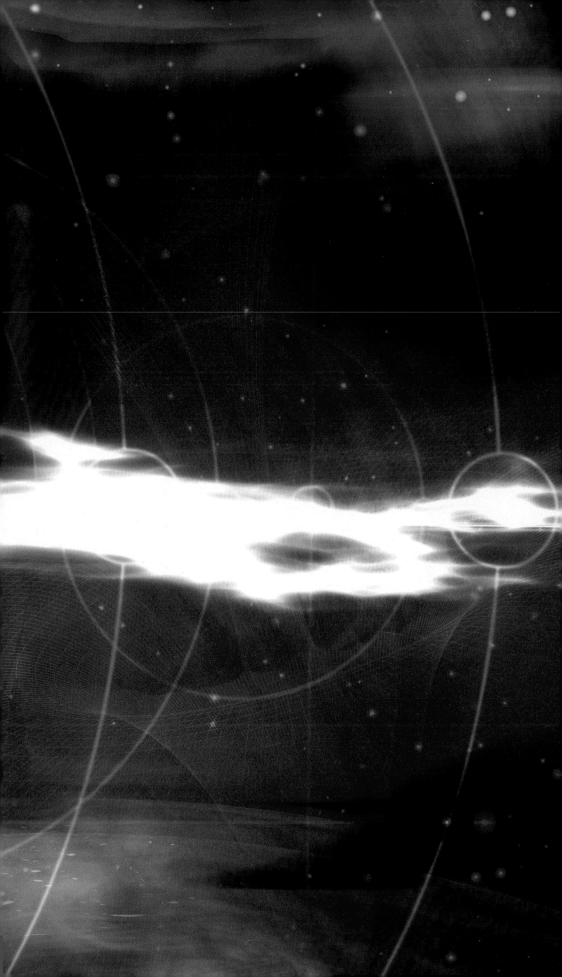

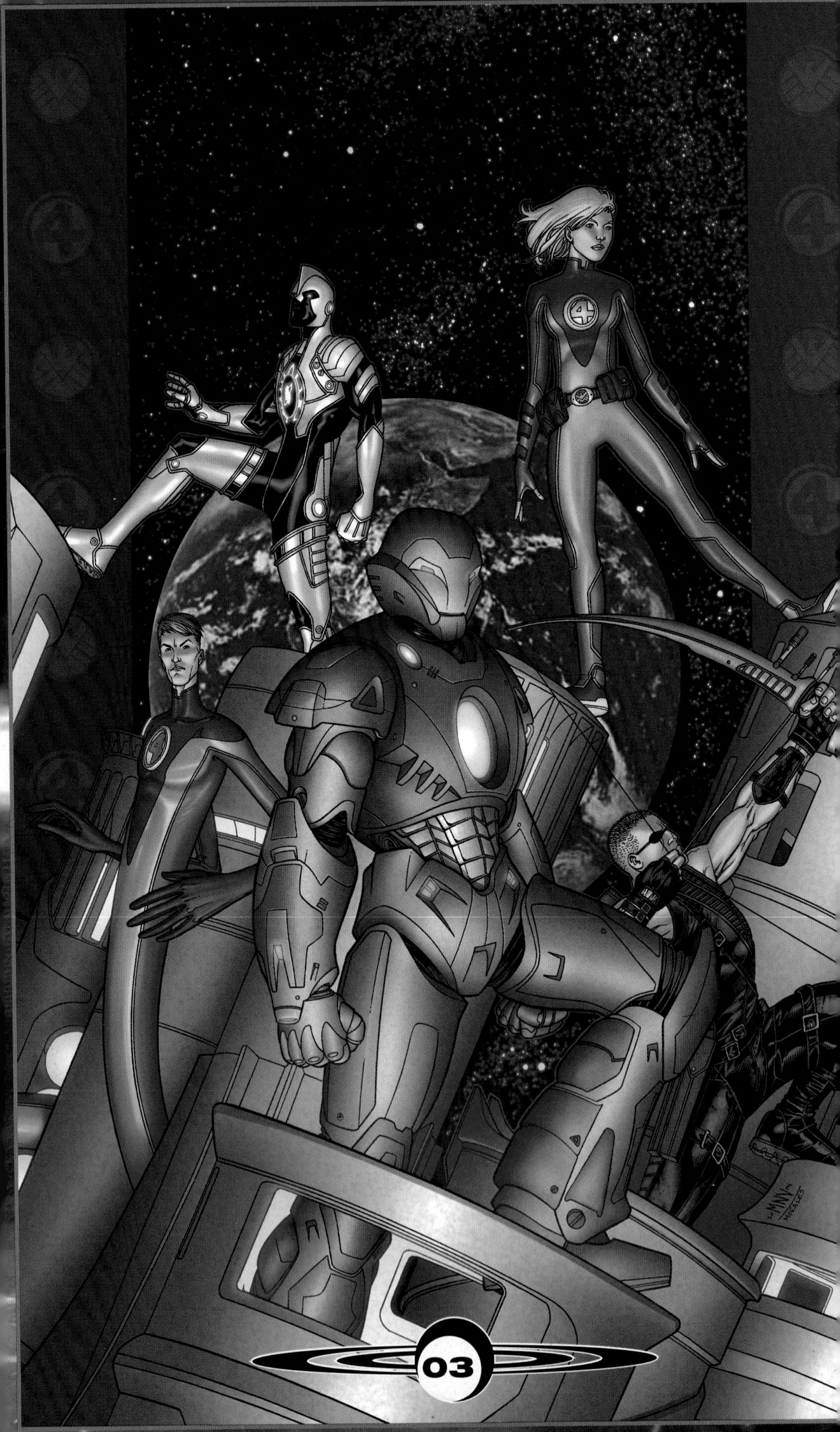
03

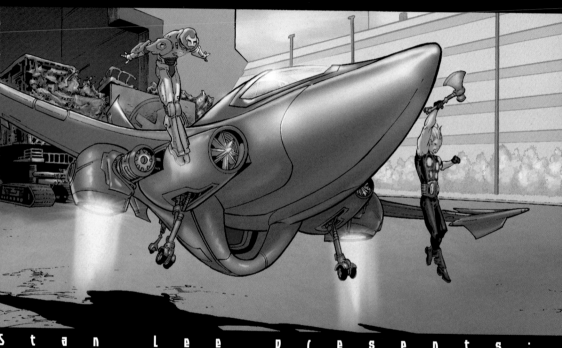

ULTIMATE SECRET

CHAPTER THREE

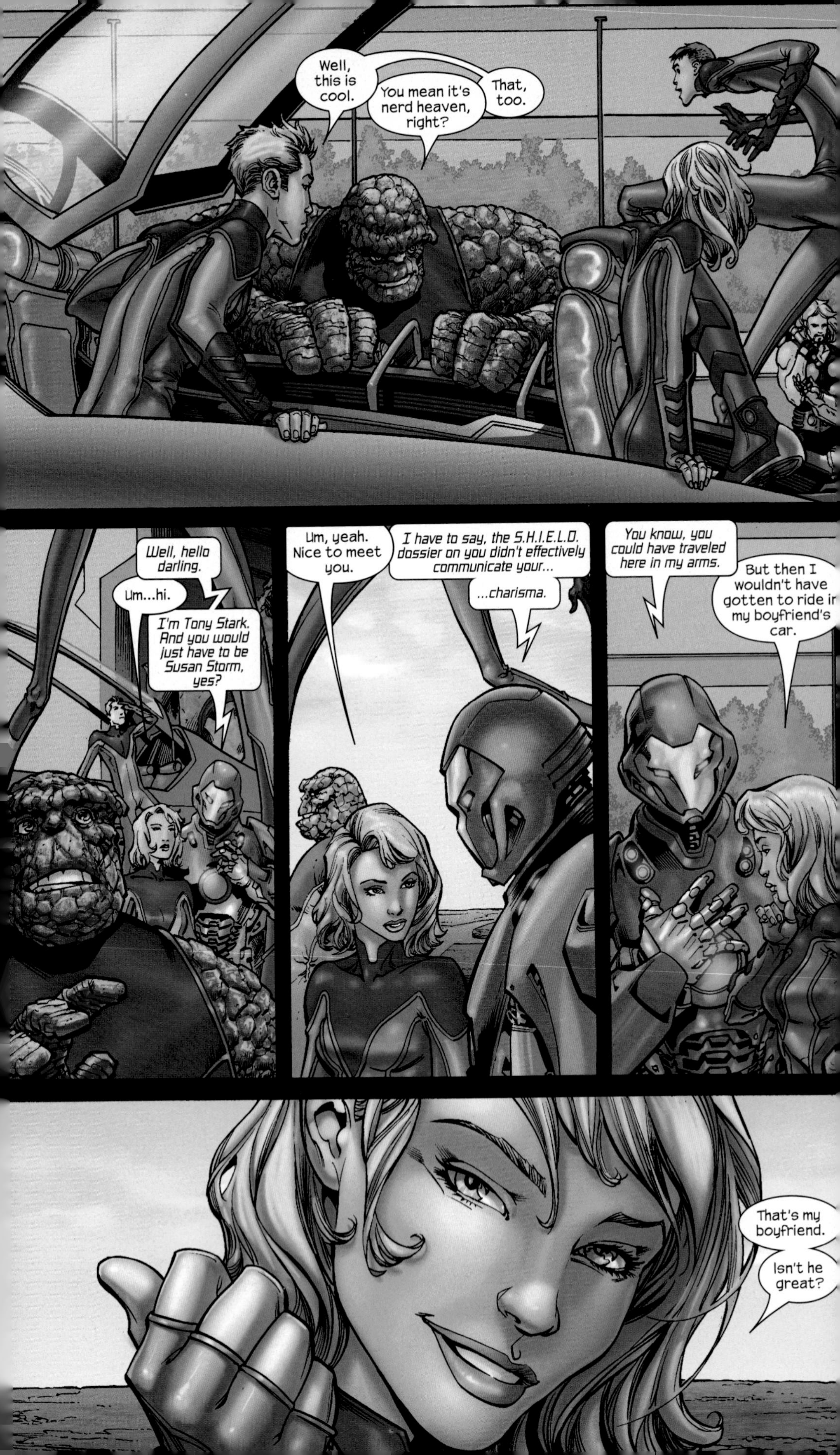

Well, this is cool.
You mean it's nerd heaven, right?
That, too.
Well, hello darling.
Um...hi.
I'm Tony Stark. And you would just have to be Susan Storm, yes?
Um, yeah. Nice to meet you.
I have to say, the S.H.I.E.L.D. dossier on you didn't effectively communicate your...
...charisma.
You know, you could have traveled here in my arms.
But then I wouldn't have gotten to ride in my boyfriend's car.
That's my boyfriend.
Isn't he great?

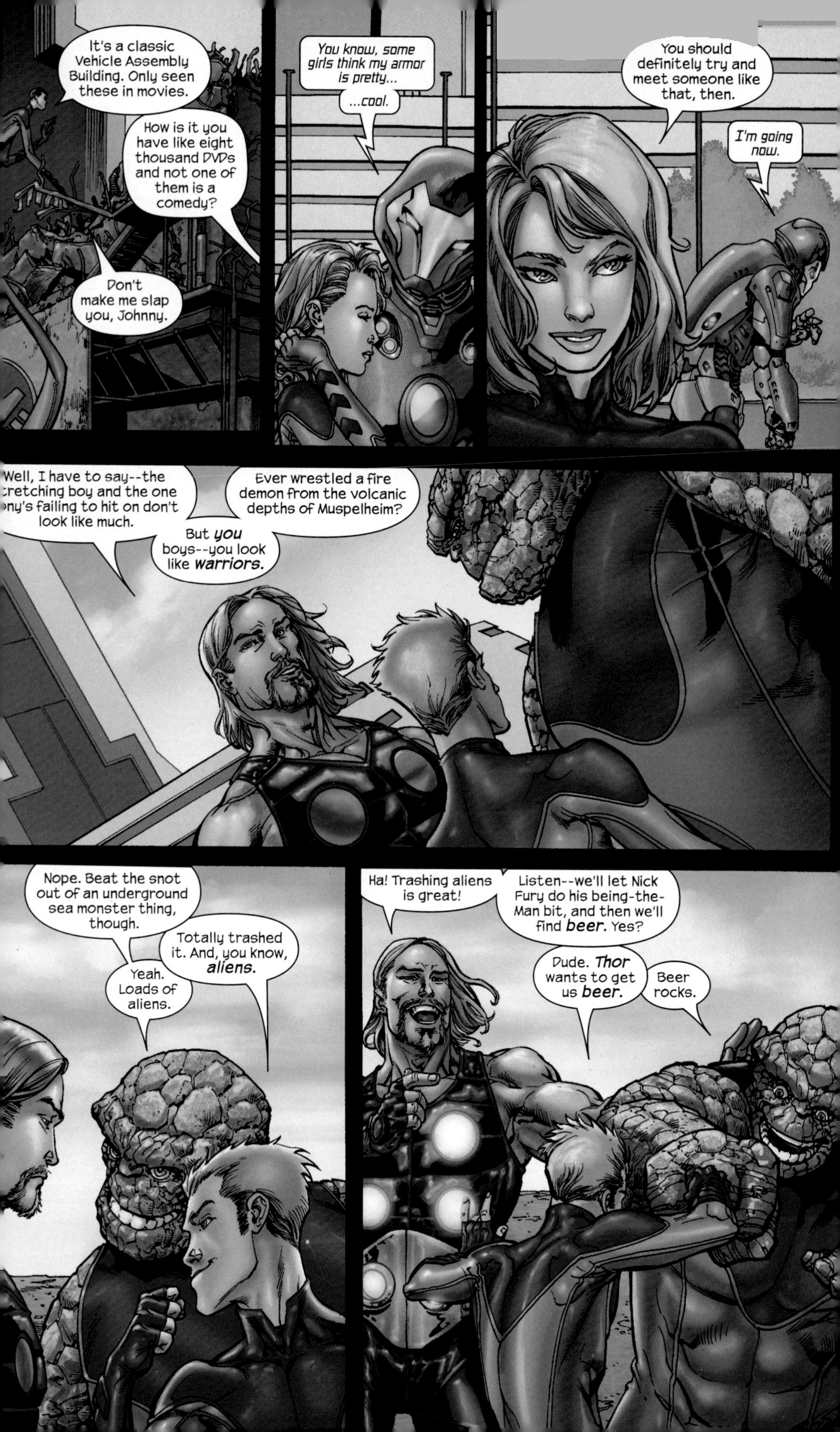

It's a classic Vehicle Assembly Building. Only seen these in movies.
How is it you have like eight thousand DVDs and not one of them is a comedy?
Don't make me slap you, Johnny.
You know, some girls think my armor is pretty...
...cool.
You should definitely try and meet someone like that, then.
I'm going now.
Well, I have to say--the
retching boy and the one
ny's failing to hit on don't look like much.
But you boys--you look like warriors.
Ever wrestled a fire demon from the volcanic depths of Muspelheim?
Nope. Beat the snot out of an underground sea monster thing, though.
Yeah. Loads of aliens.
Totally trashed it. And, you know, aliens.
Ha! Trashing aliens is great!
Listen--we'll let Nick Fury do his being-the-Man bit, and then we'll find beer. Yes?
Dude. Thor wants to get us beer.
Beer rocks.

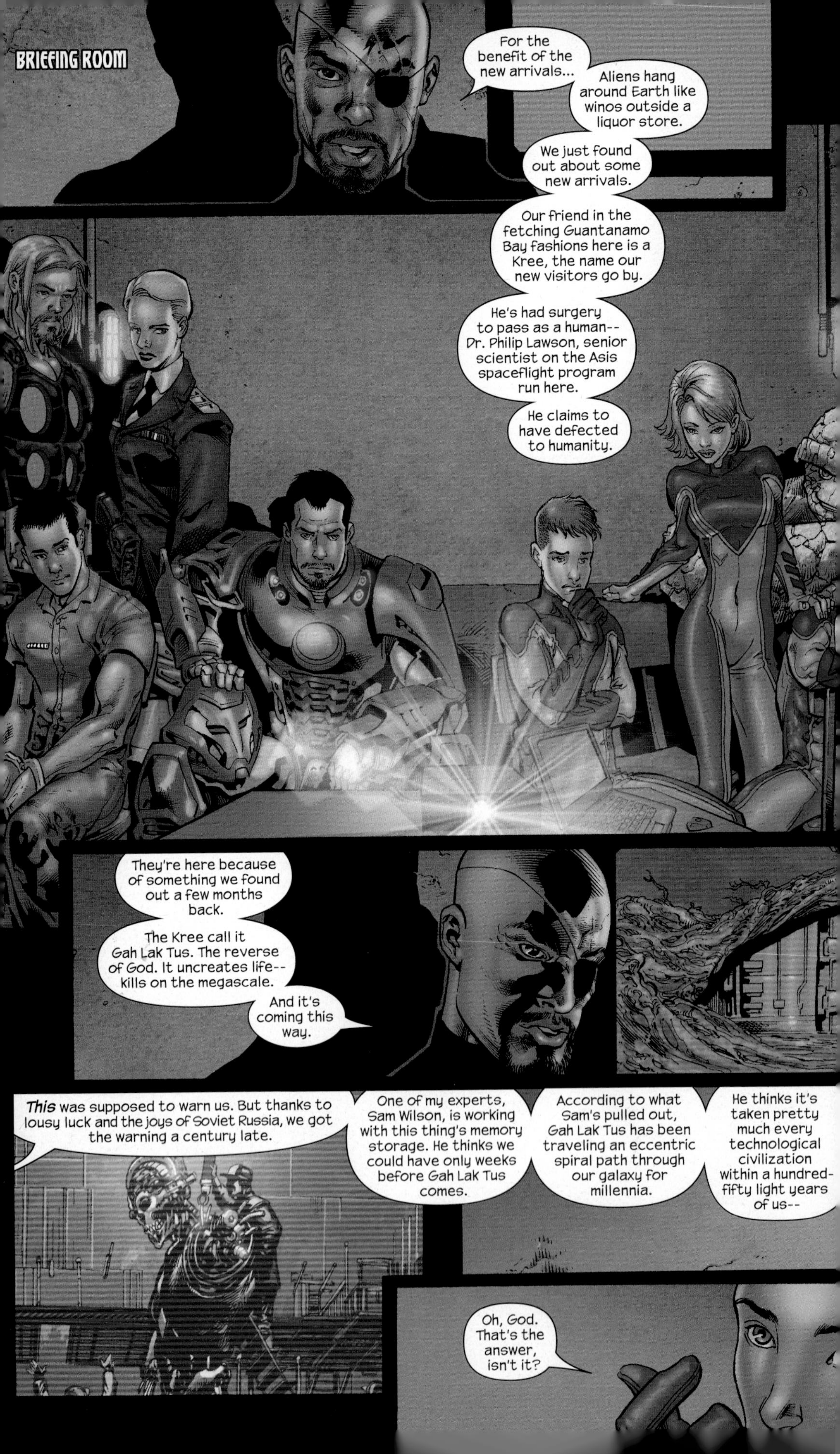
BRIEFING ROOM
For the benefit of the new arrivals...
Aliens hang around Earth like winos outside a liquor store.
We just found out about some new arrivals.
Our friend in the fetching Guantanamo Bay fashions here is a Kree, the name our new visitors go by.
He's had surgery to pass as a human-- Dr. Philip Lawson, senior scientist on the Asis spaceflight program run here.
He claims to have defected to humanity.
They're here because of something we found out a few months back.
The Kree call it Gah Lak Tus. The reverse of God. It uncreates life-- kills on the megascale.
And it's coming this way.
This was supposed to warn us. But thanks to lousy luck and the joys of Soviet Russia, we got the warning a century late.
One of my experts, Sam Wilson, is working with this thing's memory storage. He thinks we could have only weeks before Gah Lak Tus comes.
According to what Sam's pulled out, Gah Lak Tus has been traveling an eccentric spiral path through our galaxy for millennia.
He thinks it's taken pretty much every technological civilization within a hundred-fifty light years of us--
Oh, God. That's the answer, isn't it?

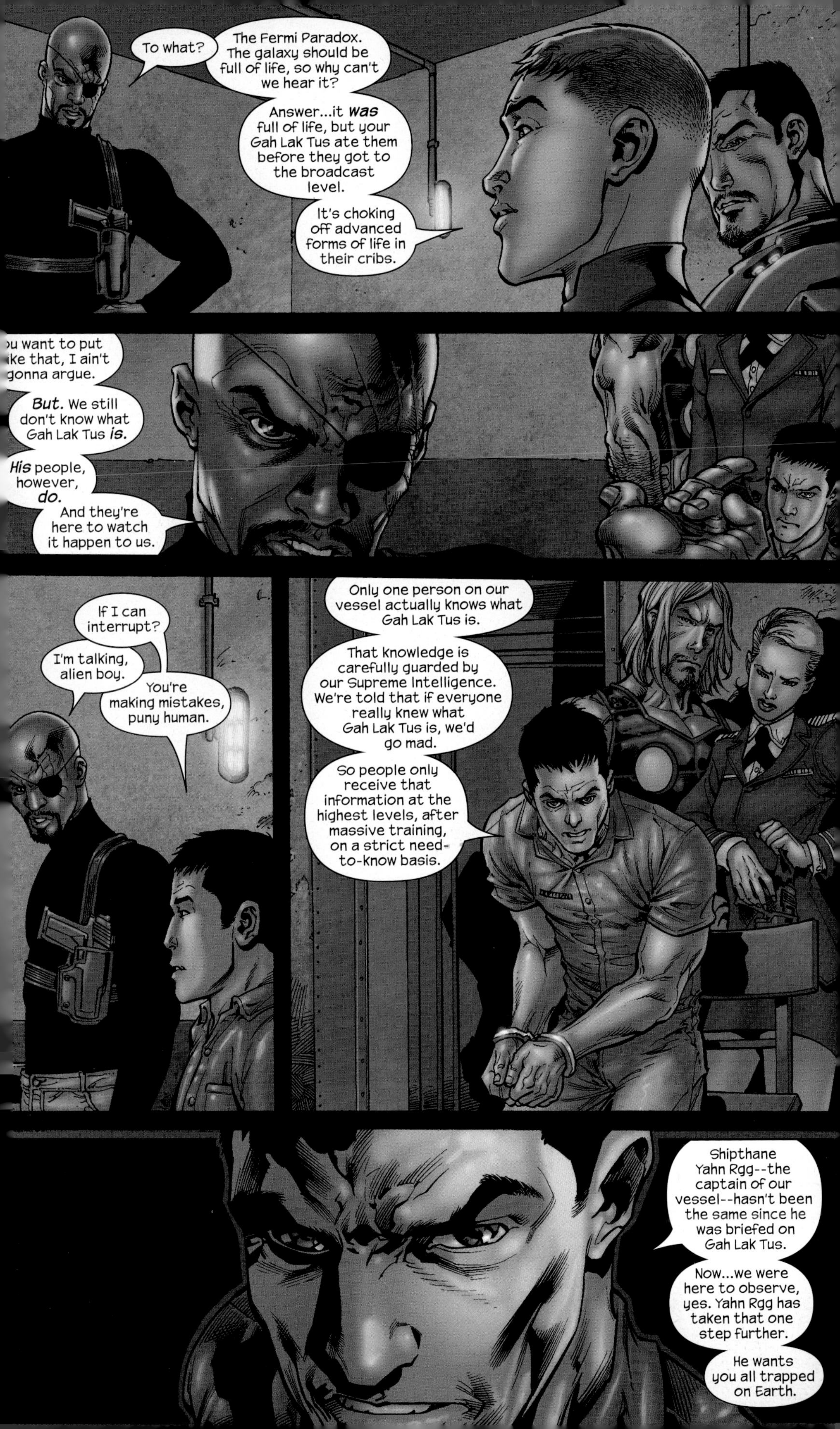

To what?
The Fermi Paradox. The galaxy should be full of life, so why can't we hear it?
Answer...it *was* full of life, but your Gah Lak Tus ate them before they got to the broadcast level.
It's choking off advanced forms of life in their cribs.
ou want to put ike that, I ain't gonna argue.
But. We still don't know what Gah Lak Tus *is.*
His people, however, *do.*
And they're here to watch it happen to us.
If I can interrupt?
I'm talking, alien boy.
You're making mistakes, puny human.
Only one person on our vessel actually knows what Gah Lak Tus is.
That knowledge is carefully guarded by our Supreme Intelligence. We're told that if everyone really knew what Gah Lak Tus is, we'd go mad.
So people only receive that information at the highest levels, after massive training, on a strict need-to-know basis.
Shipthane Yahn Rgg--the captain of our vessel--hasn't been the same since he was briefed on Gah Lak Tus.
Now...we were here to observe, yes. Yahn Rgg has taken that one step further.
He wants you all trapped on Earth.

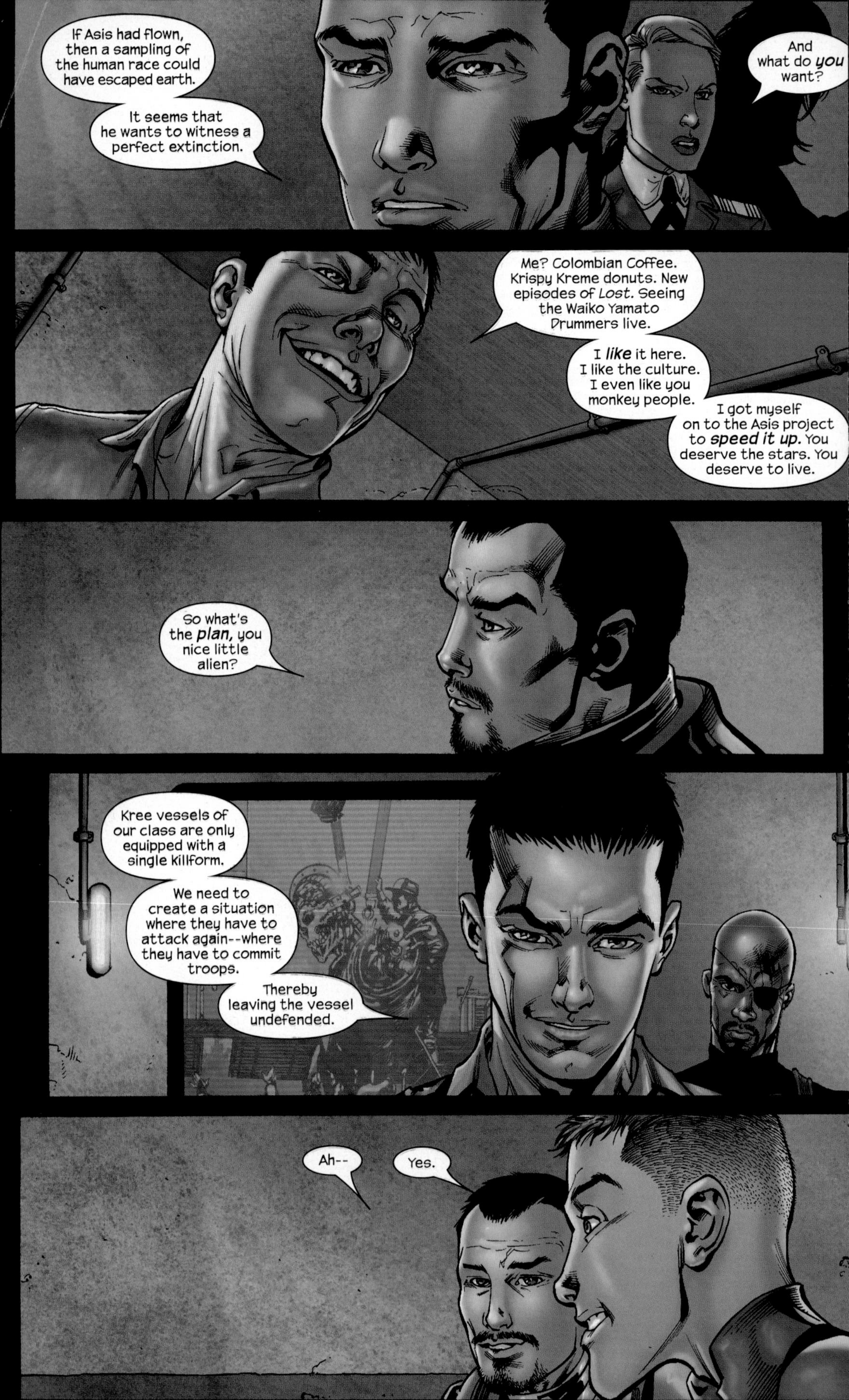

If Asis had flown, then a sampling of the human race could have escaped earth.
It seems that he wants to witness a perfect extinction.
And what do *you* want?
Me? Colombian Coffee. Krispy Kreme donuts. New episodes of *Lost*. Seeing the Waiko Yamato Drummers live.
I *like* it here. I like the culture. I even like you monkey people.
I got myself on to the Asis project to *speed it up*. You deserve the stars. You deserve to live.
So what's the *plan*, you nice little alien?
Kree vessels of our class are only equipped with a single killform.
We need to create a situation where they have to attack again--where they have to commit troops.
Thereby leaving the vessel undefended.
Ah--
Yes.

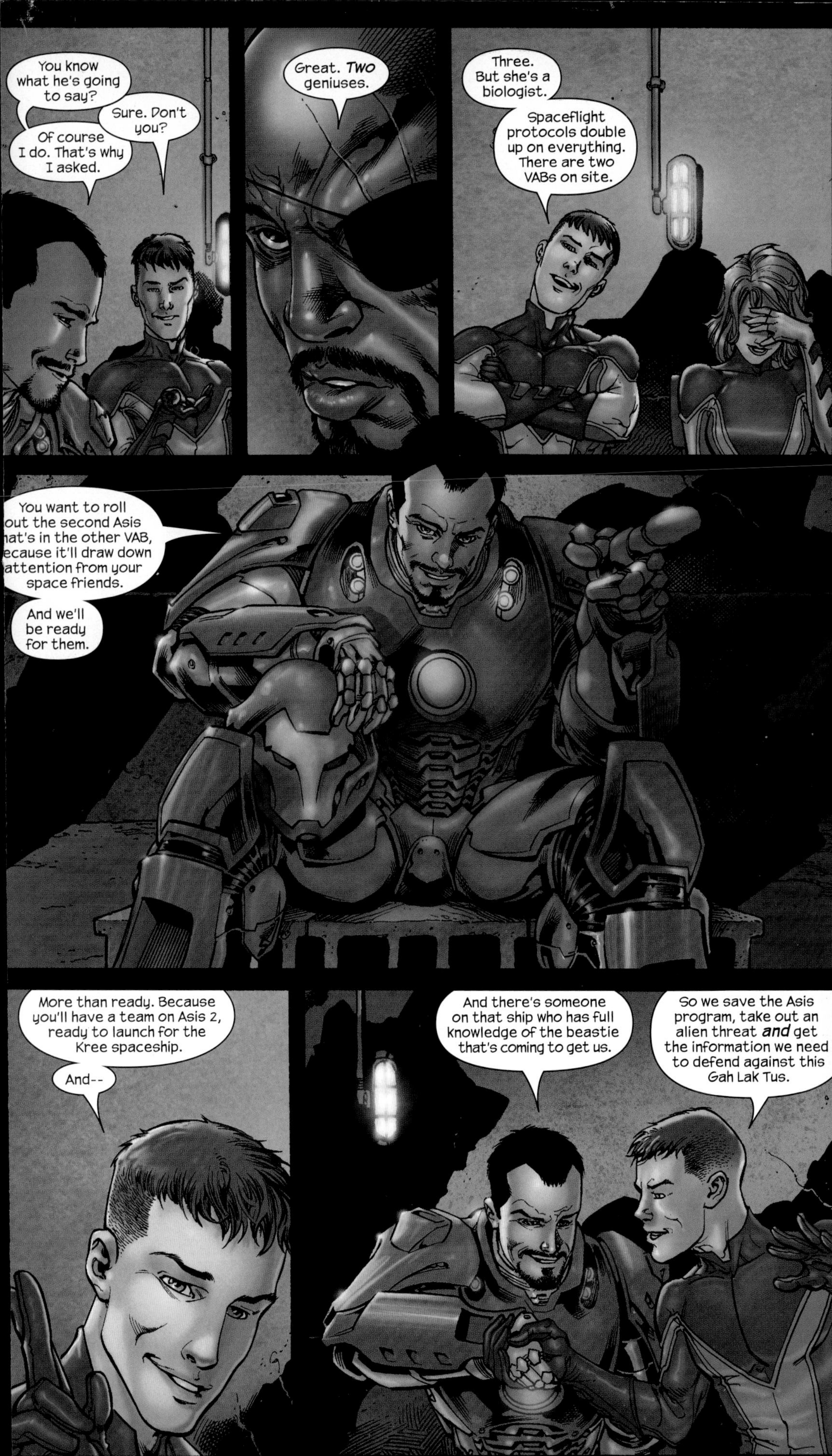
You know what he's going to say?
Sure. Don't you?
Of course I do. That's why I asked.
Great. TWO geniuses.
Three. But she's a biologist.
Spaceflight protocols double up on everything. There are two VABs on site.
You want to roll out the second Asis that's in the other VAB, because it'll draw down attention from your space friends.
And we'll be ready for them.
More than ready. Because you'll have a team on Asis 2, ready to launch for the Kree spaceship.
And--
And there's someone on that ship who has full knowledge of the beastie that's coming to get us.
So we save the Asis program, take out an alien threat and get the information we need to defend against this Gah Lak Tus.

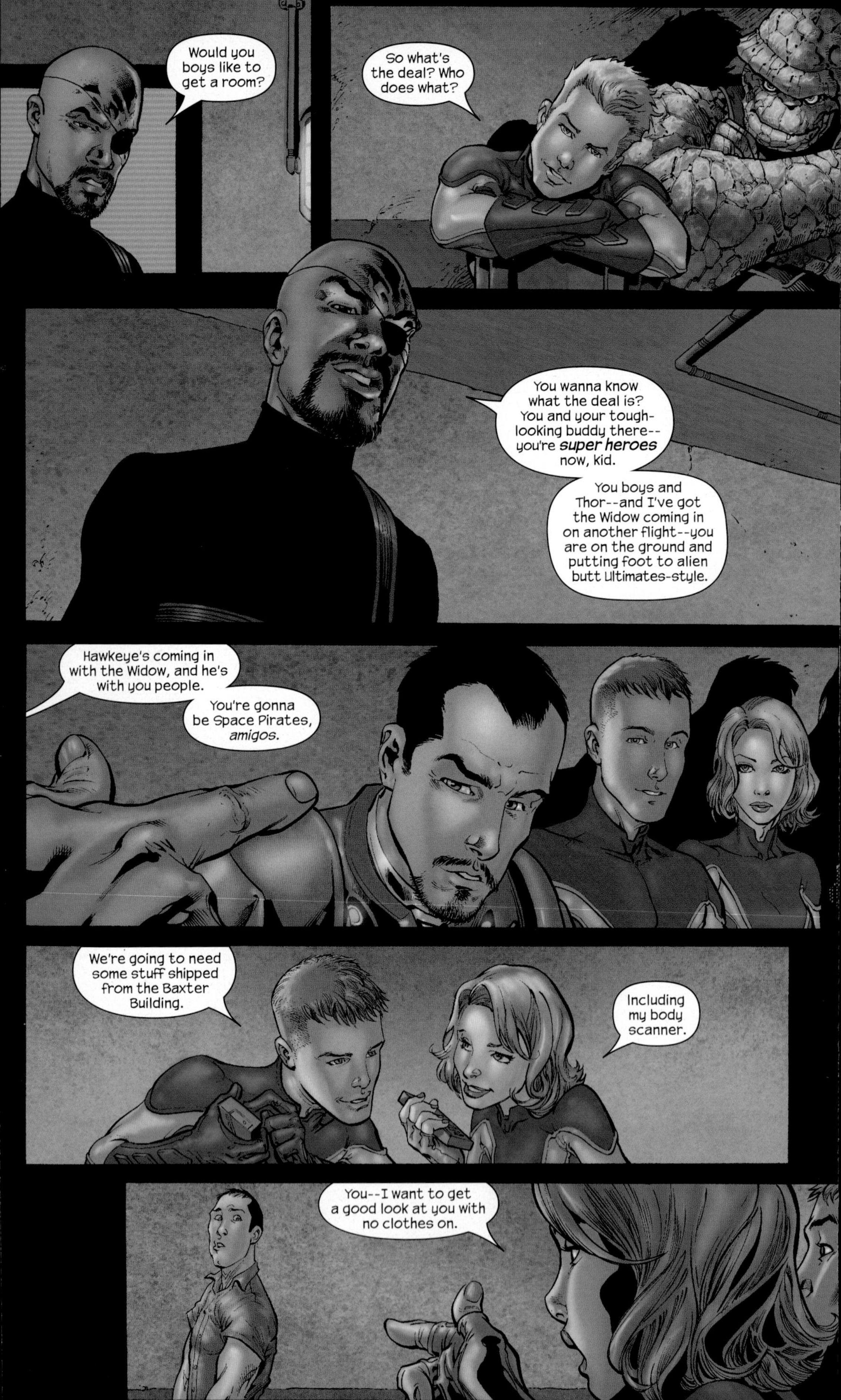

Would you boys like to get a room?
So what's the deal? Who does what?
You wanna know what the deal is? You and your tough-looking buddy there--you're *super heroes* now, kid.
You boys and Thor--and I've got the Widow coming in on another flight--you are on the ground and putting foot to alien butt Ultimates-style.
Hawkeye's coming in with the Widow, and he's with you people.
You're gonna be Space Pirates, *amigos.*
We're going to need some stuff shipped from the Baxter Building.
Including my body scanner.
You--I want to get a good look at you with no clothes on.

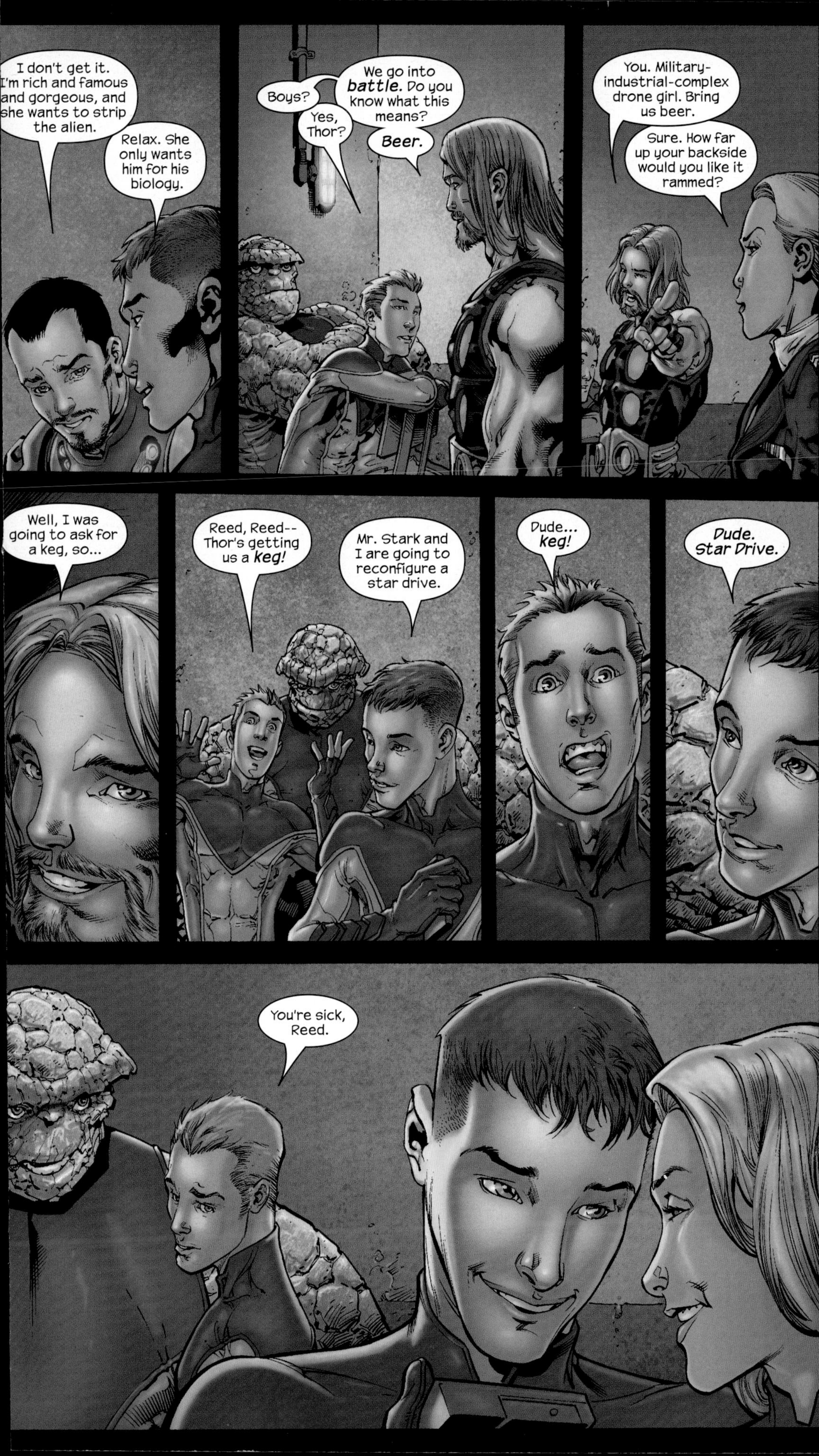
I don't get it. I'm rich and famous and gorgeous, and she wants to strip the alien.
Relax. She only wants him for his biology.
Boys?
Yes, Thor?
We go into battle. Do you know what this means?
Beer.
You. Military-industrial-complex drone girl. Bring us beer.
Sure. How far up your backside would you like it rammed?
Well, I was going to ask for a keg, so...
Reed, Reed-- Thor's getting us a keg!
Mr. Stark and I are going to reconfigure a star drive.
Dude... keg!
Dude. Star Drive.
You're sick, Reed.

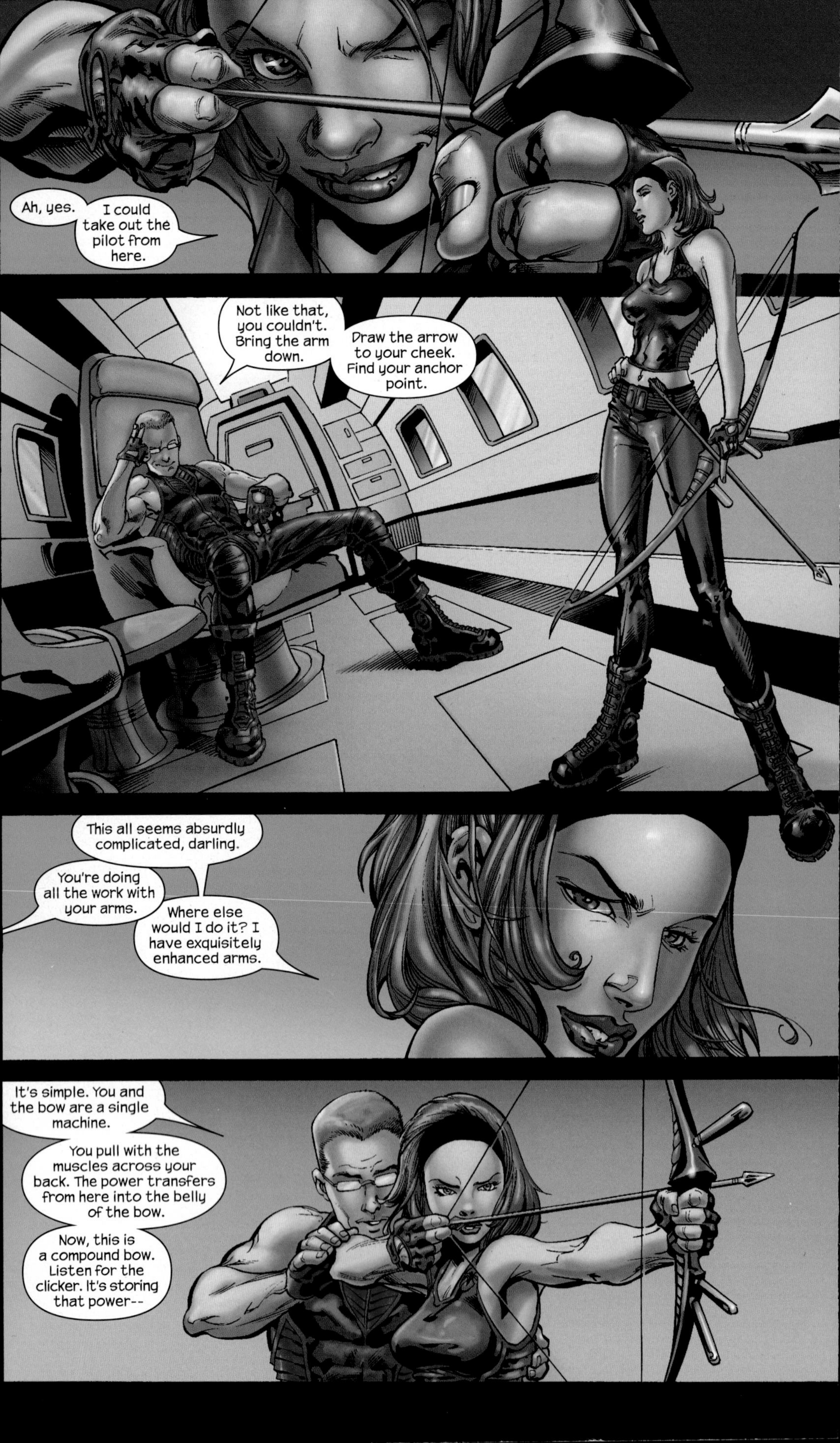

Ah, yes.
I could take out the pilot from here.
Not like that, you couldn't. Bring the arm down.
Draw the arrow to your cheek. Find your anchor point.
This all seems absurdly complicated, darling.
You're doing all the work with your arms.
Where else would I do it? I have exquisitely enhanced arms.
It's simple. You and the bow are a single machine.
You pull with the muscles across your back. The power transfers from here into the belly of the bow.
Now, this is a compound bow. Listen for the clicker. It's storing that power--

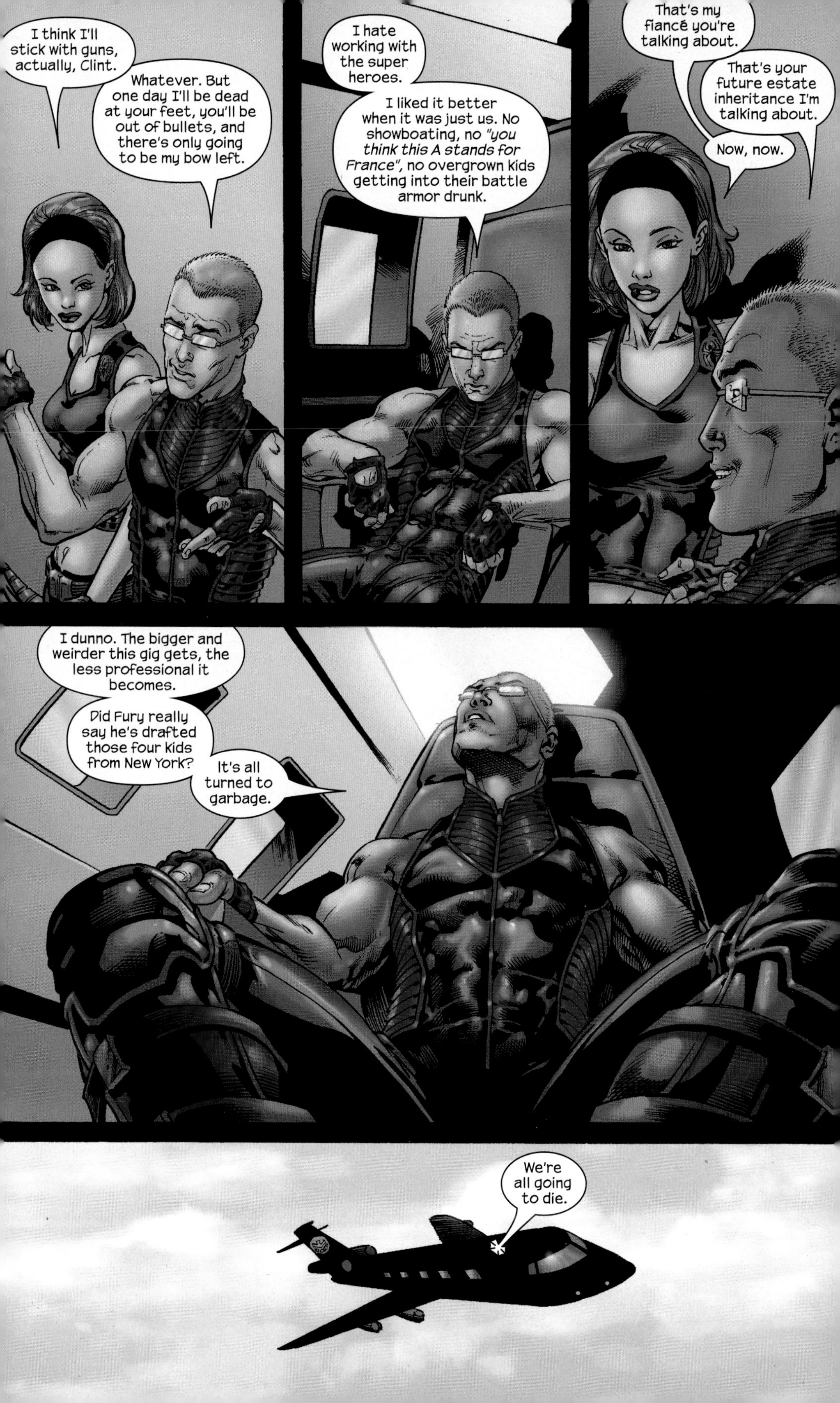
I think I'll stick with guns, actually, Clint.
Whatever. But one day I'll be dead at your feet, you'll be out of bullets, and there's only going to be my bow left.
I hate working with the super heroes.
I liked it better when it was just us. No showboating, no "you think this A stands for France", no overgrown kids getting into their battle armor drunk.
That's my fiancé you're talking about.
That's your future estate inheritance I'm talking about.
Now, now.
I dunno. The bigger and weirder this gig gets, the less professional it becomes.
Did Fury really say he's drafted those four kids from New York?
It's all turned to garbage.
We're all going to die.

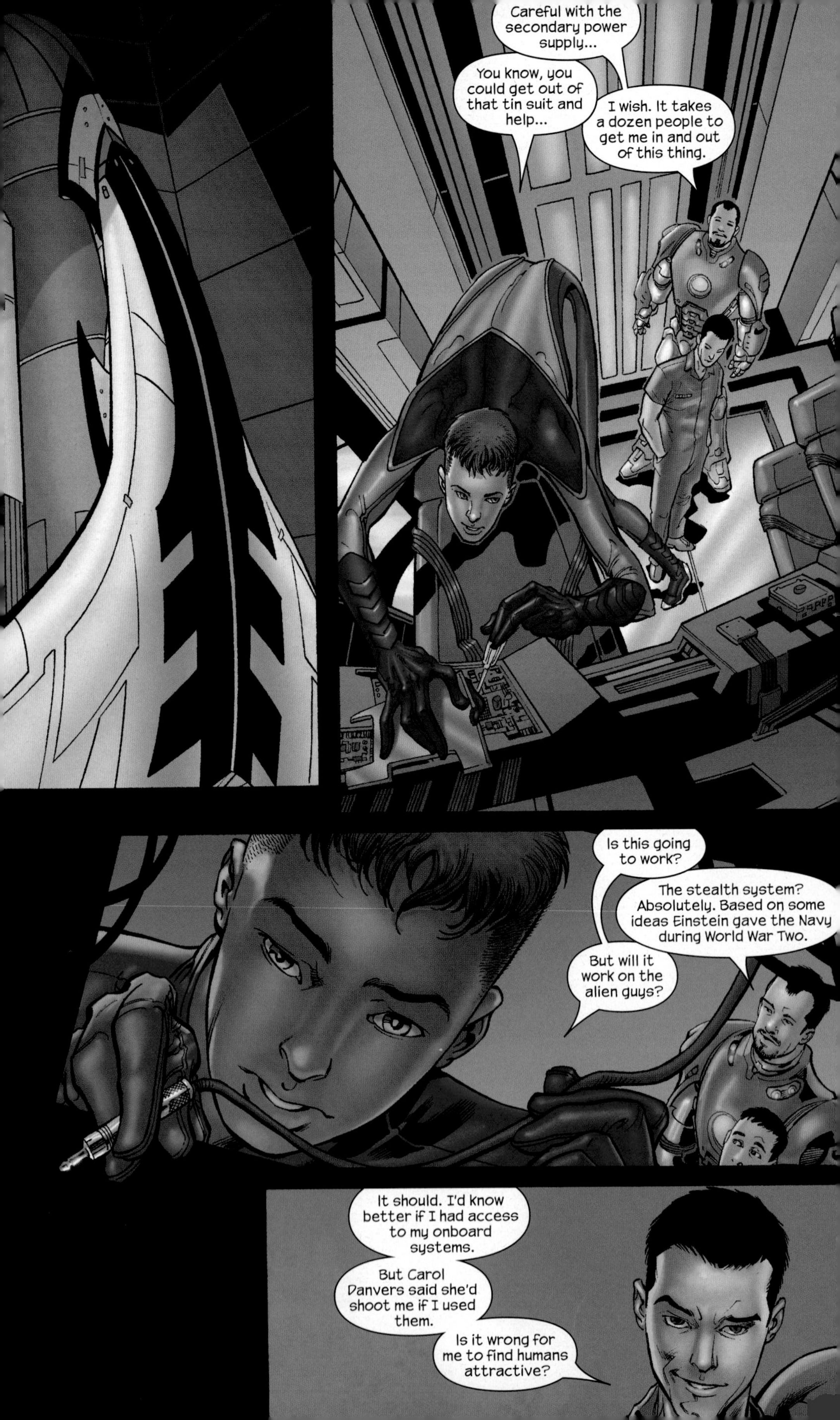
Careful with the secondary power supply...
You know, you could get out of that tin suit and help...
I wish. It takes a dozen people to get me in and out of this thing.
Is this going to work?
The stealth system? Absolutely. Based on some ideas Einstein gave the Navy during World War Two.
But will it work on the alien guys?
It should. I'd know better if I had access to my onboard systems.
But Carol Danvers said she'd shoot me if I used them.
Is it wrong for me to find humans attractive?

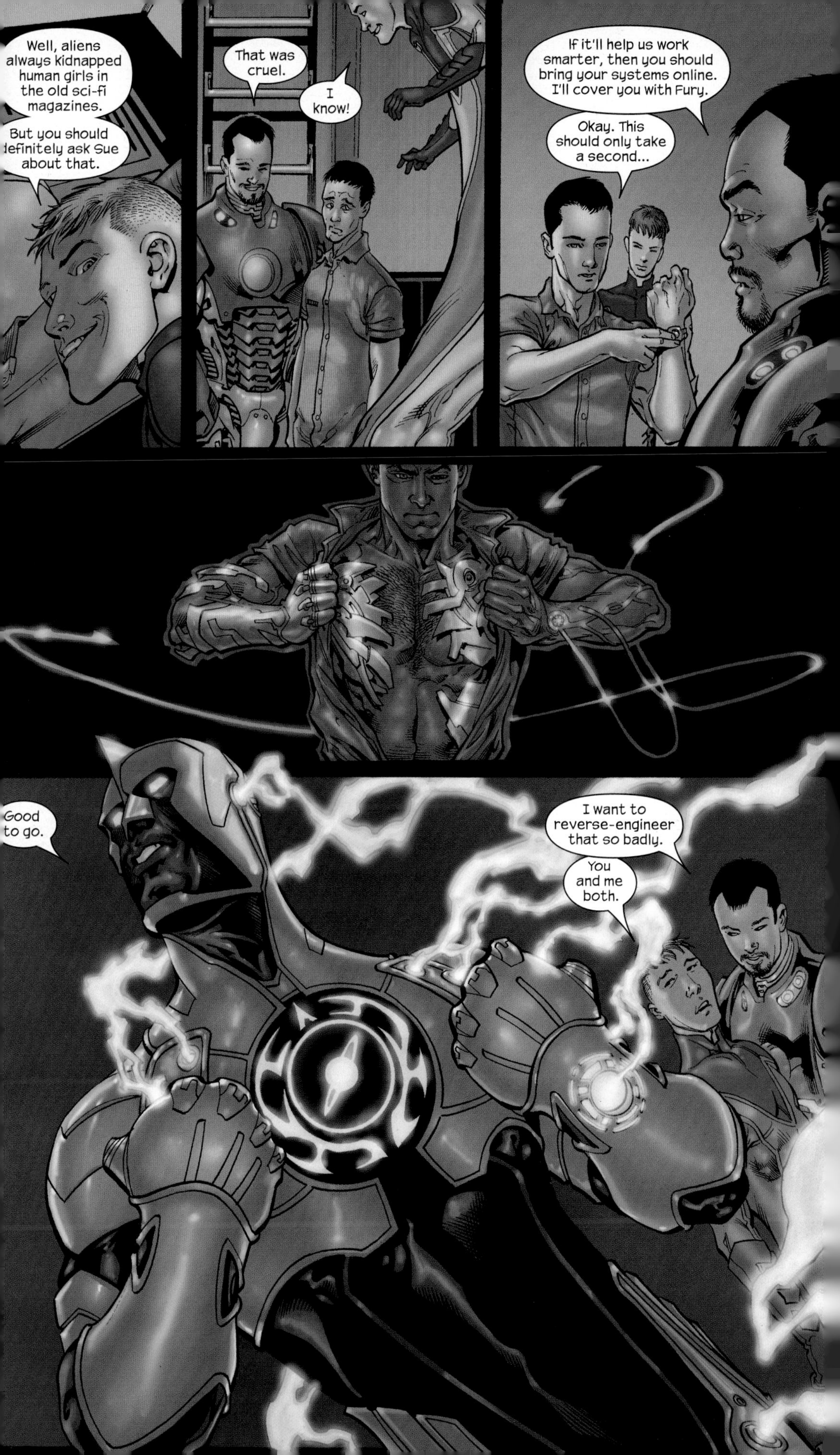
Well, aliens always kidnapped human girls in the old sci-fi magazines.
But you should definitely ask Sue about that.
That was cruel.
I know!
If it'll help us work smarter, then you should bring your systems online. I'll cover you with Fury.
Okay. This should only take a second...
Good to go.
I want to reverse-engineer that so badly.
You and me both.

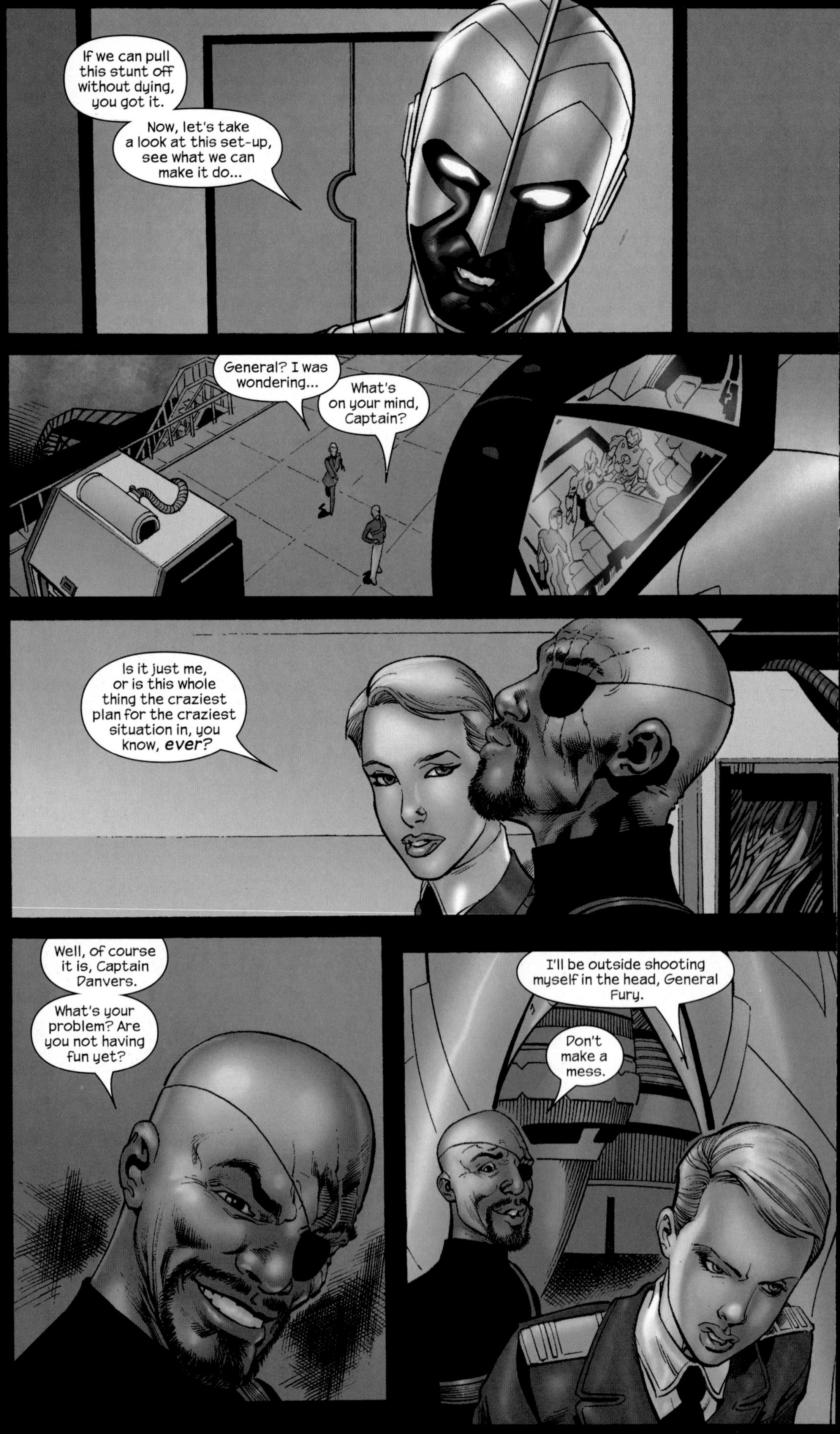

If we can pull this stunt off without dying, you got it.
Now, let's take a look at this set-up, see what we can make it do...
General? I was wondering...
What's on your mind, Captain?
Is it just me, or is this whole thing the craziest plan for the craziest situation in, you know, *ever?*
Well, of course it is, Captain Danvers.
What's your problem? Are you not having fun yet?
I'll be outside shooting myself in the head, General Fury.
Don't make a mess.

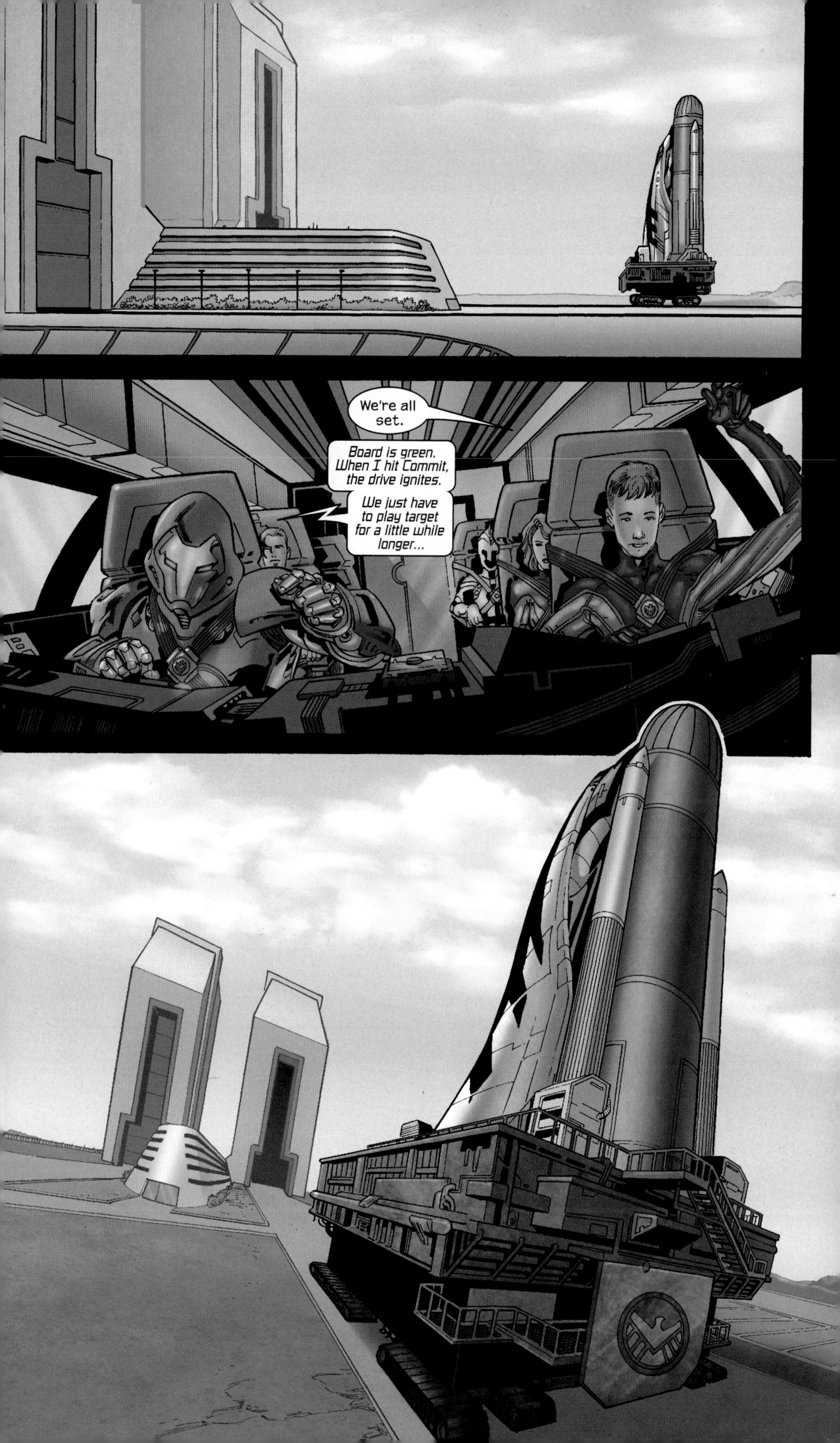
We're all set.
Board is green. When I hit Commit, the drive ignites.
We just have to play target for a little while longer...

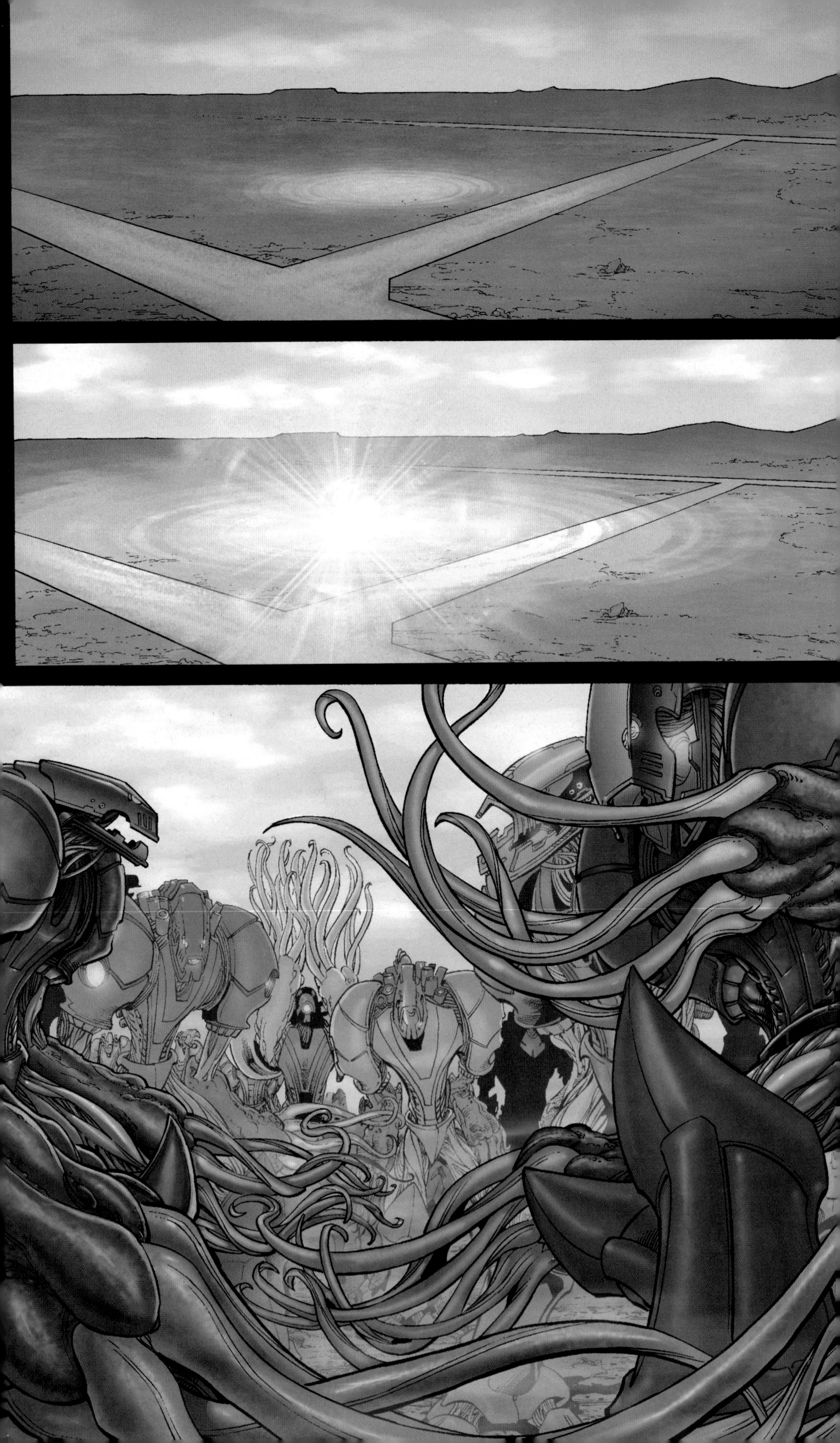

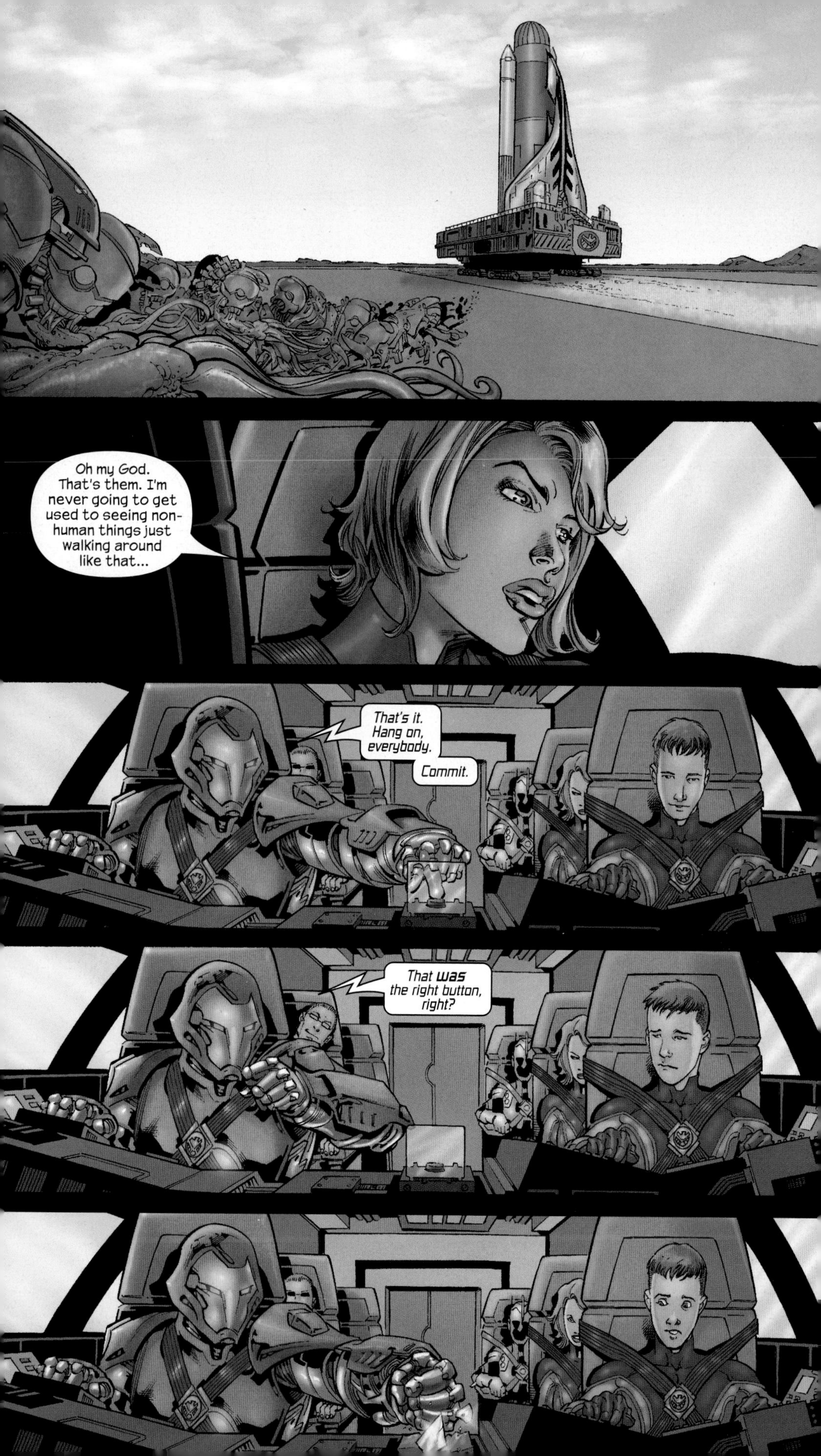

Oh my God. That's them. I'm never going to get used to seeing non-human things just walking around like that...
That's it. Hang on, everybody.
Commit.
That **WAS** the right button, right?

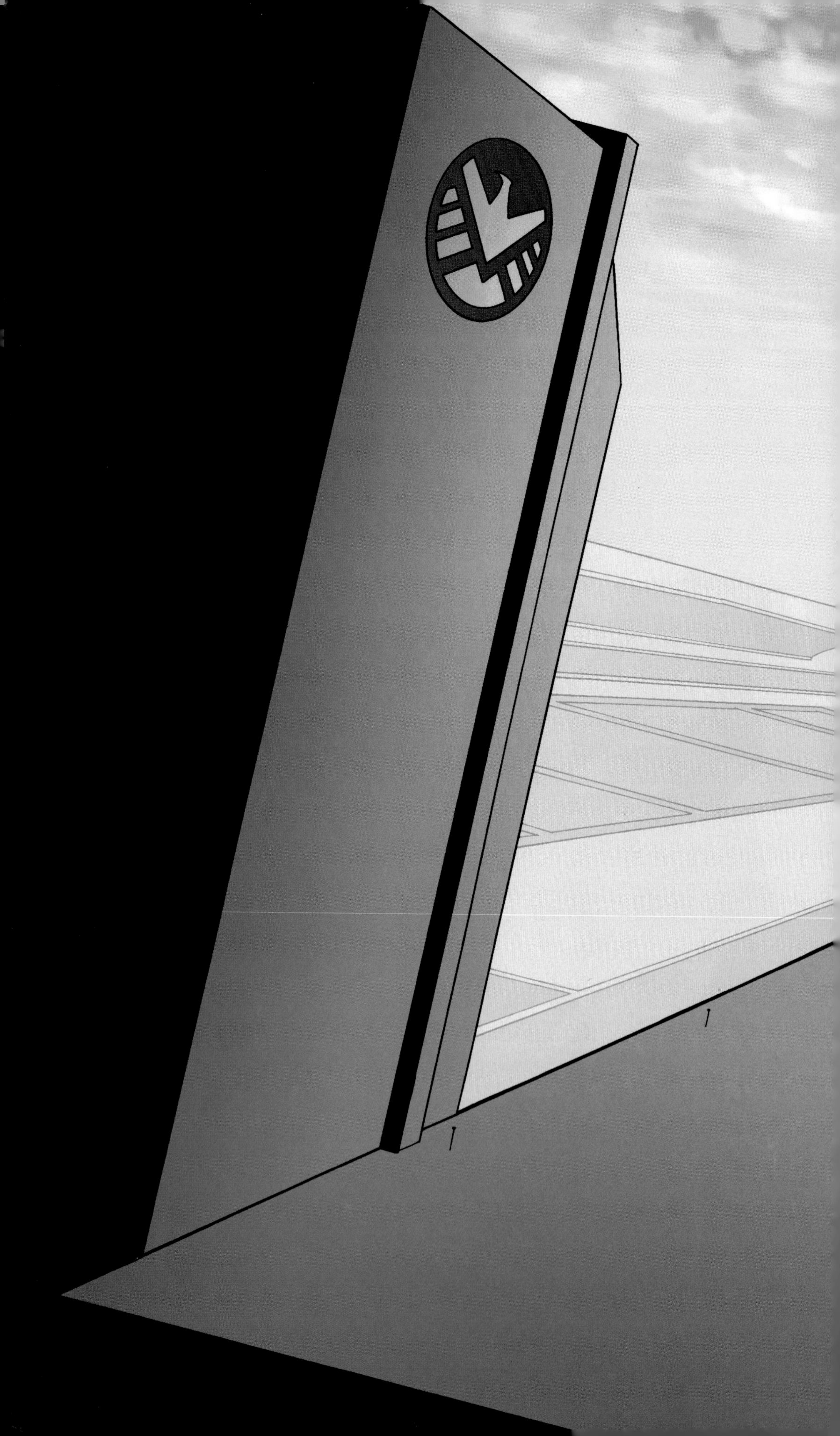

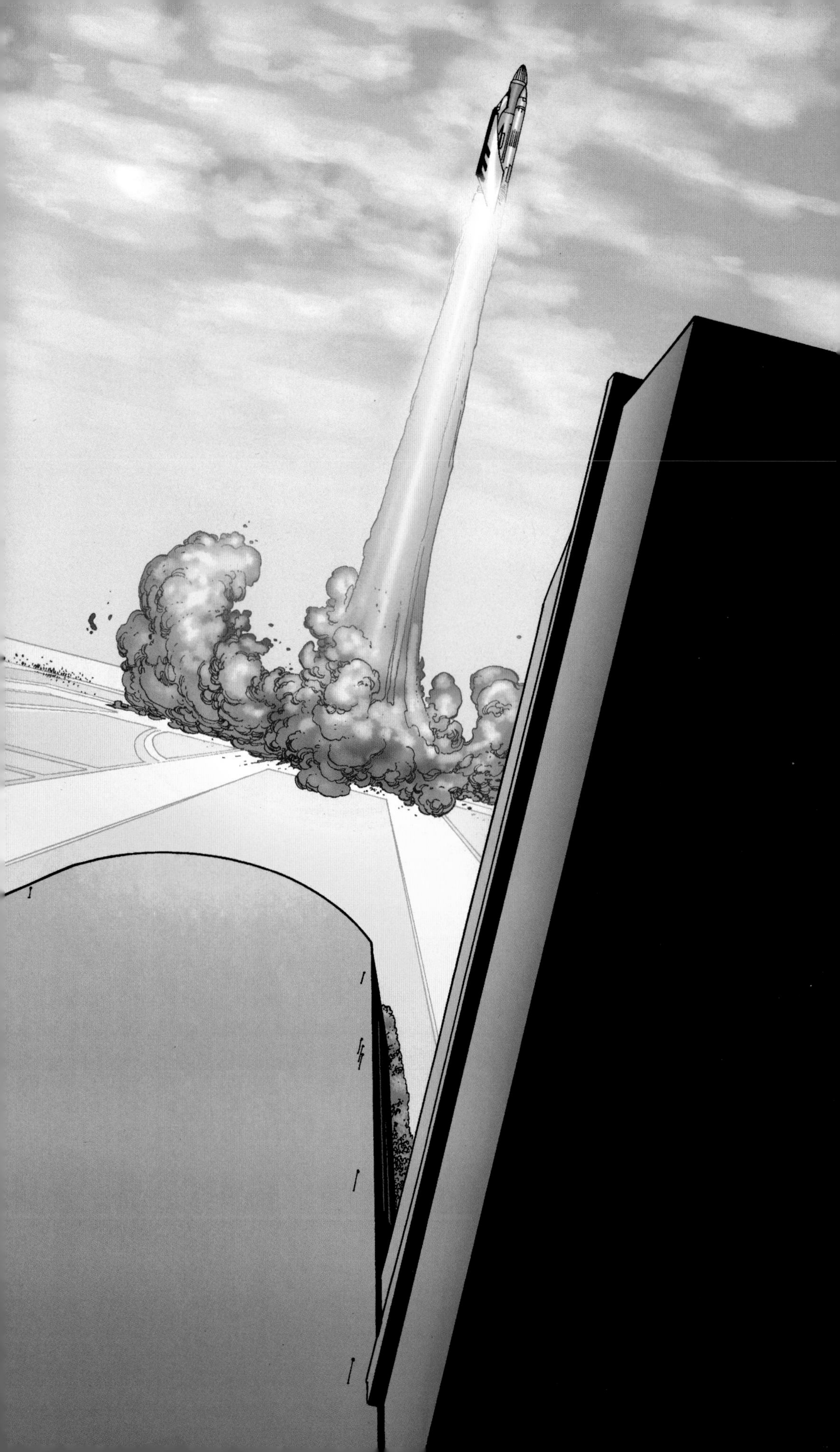

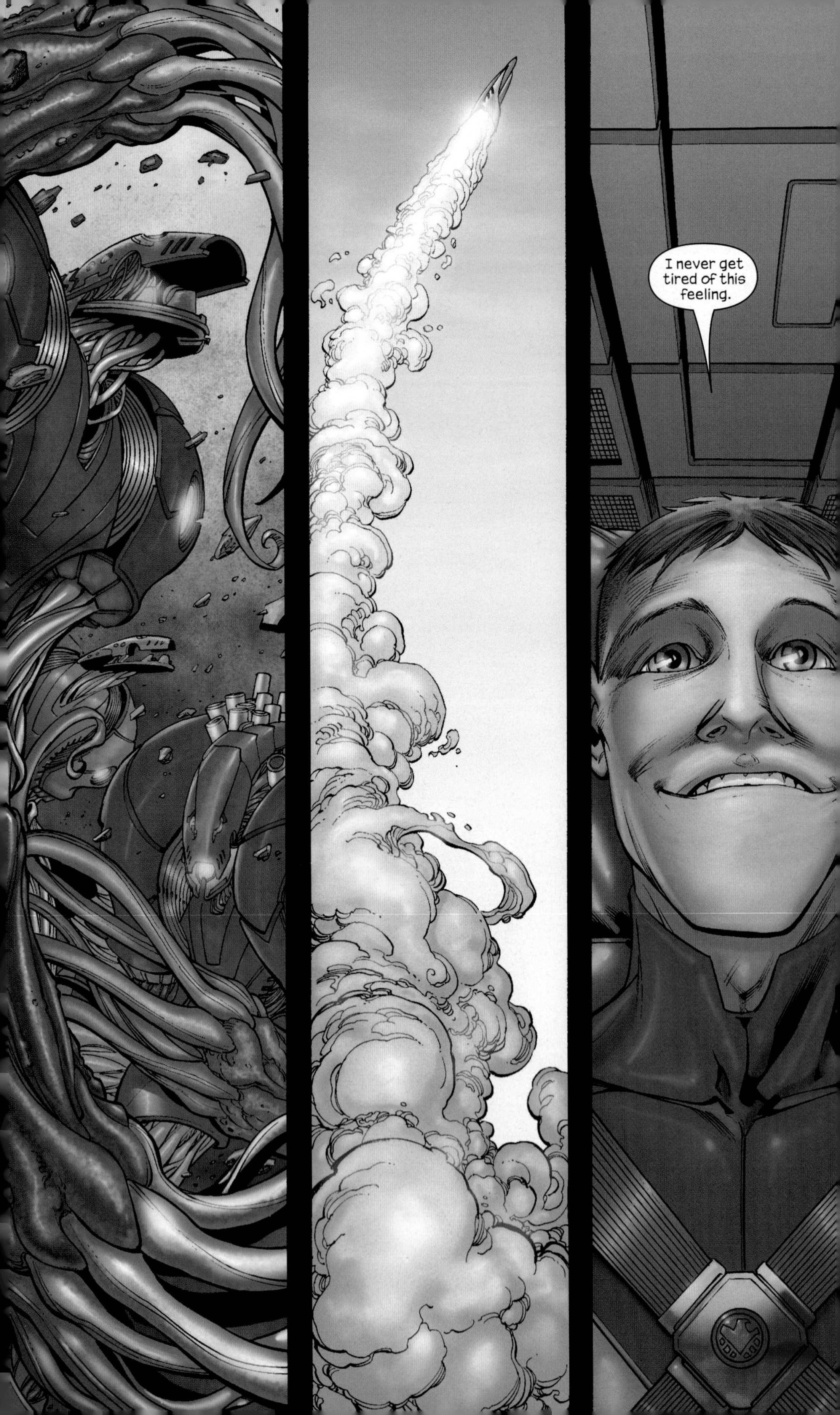
I never get tired of this feeling.

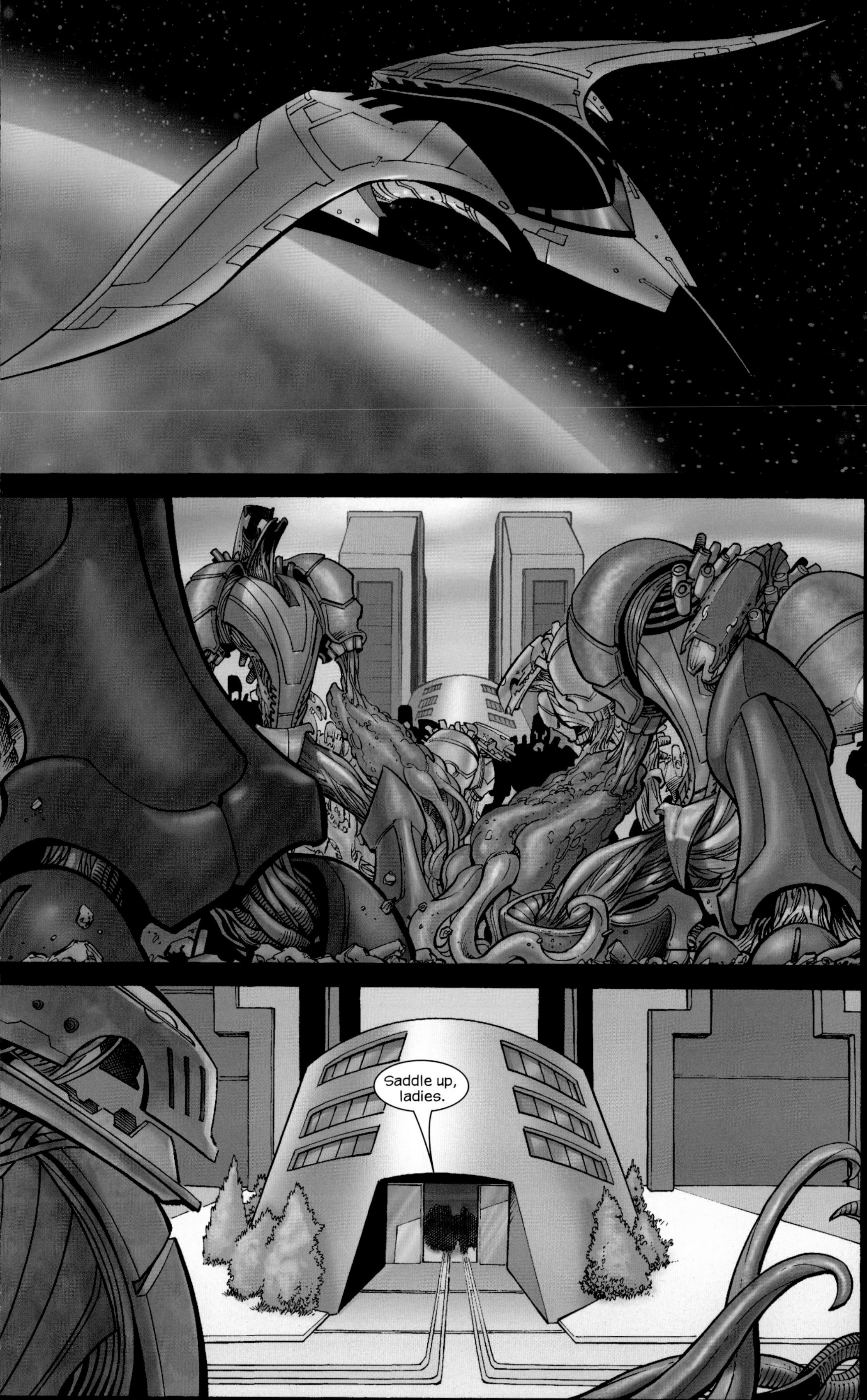
Saddle up, ladies.

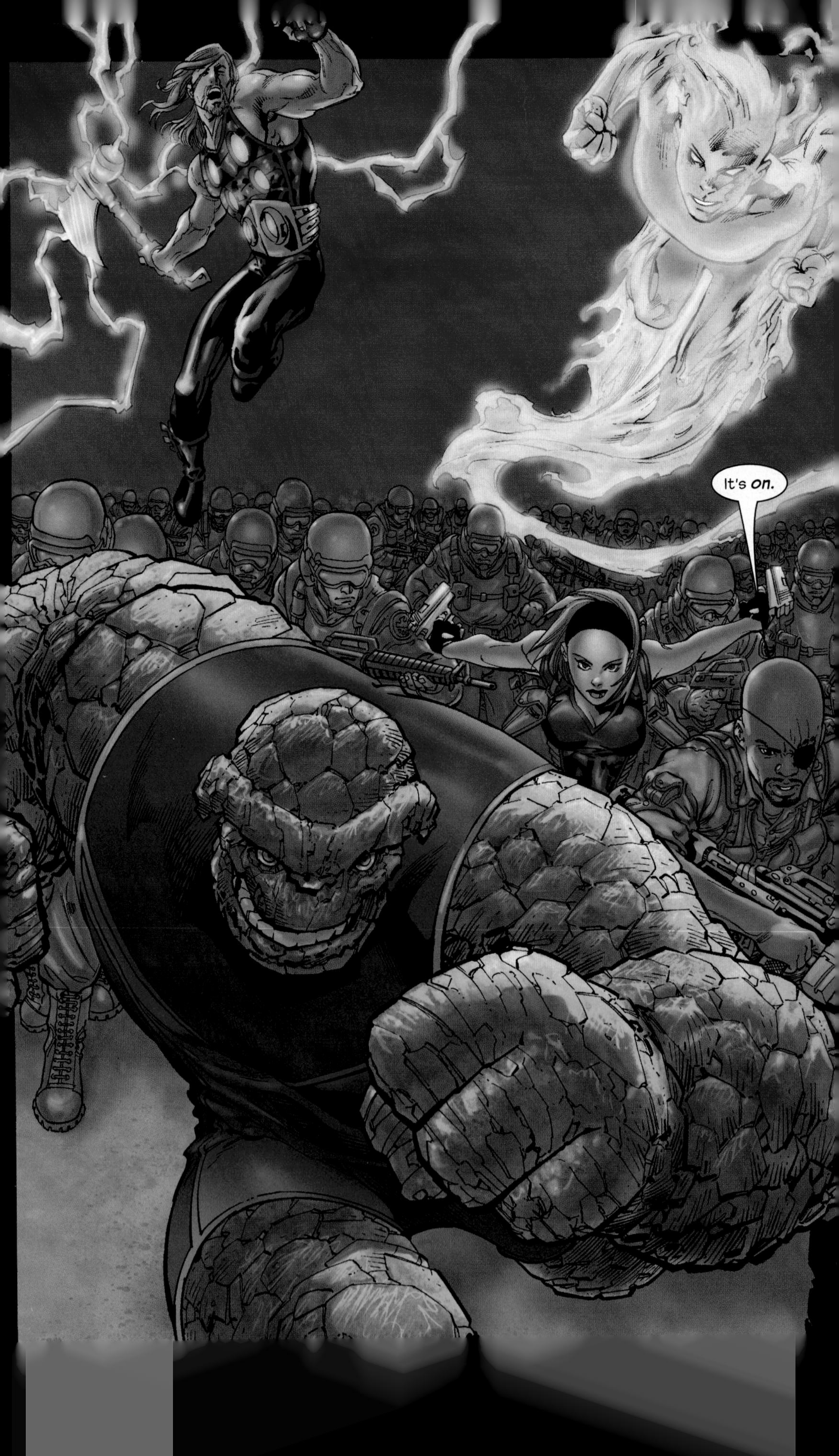
It's *on.*

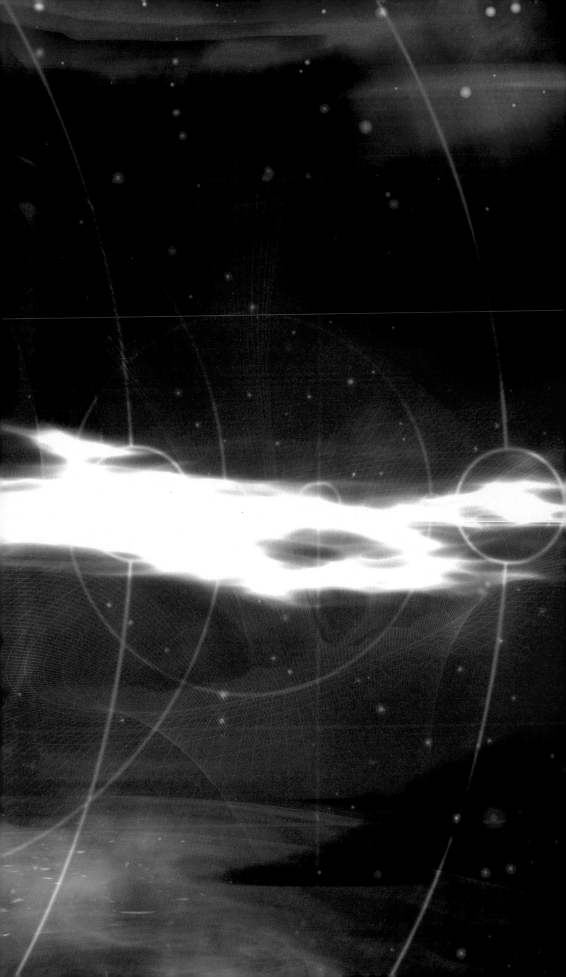

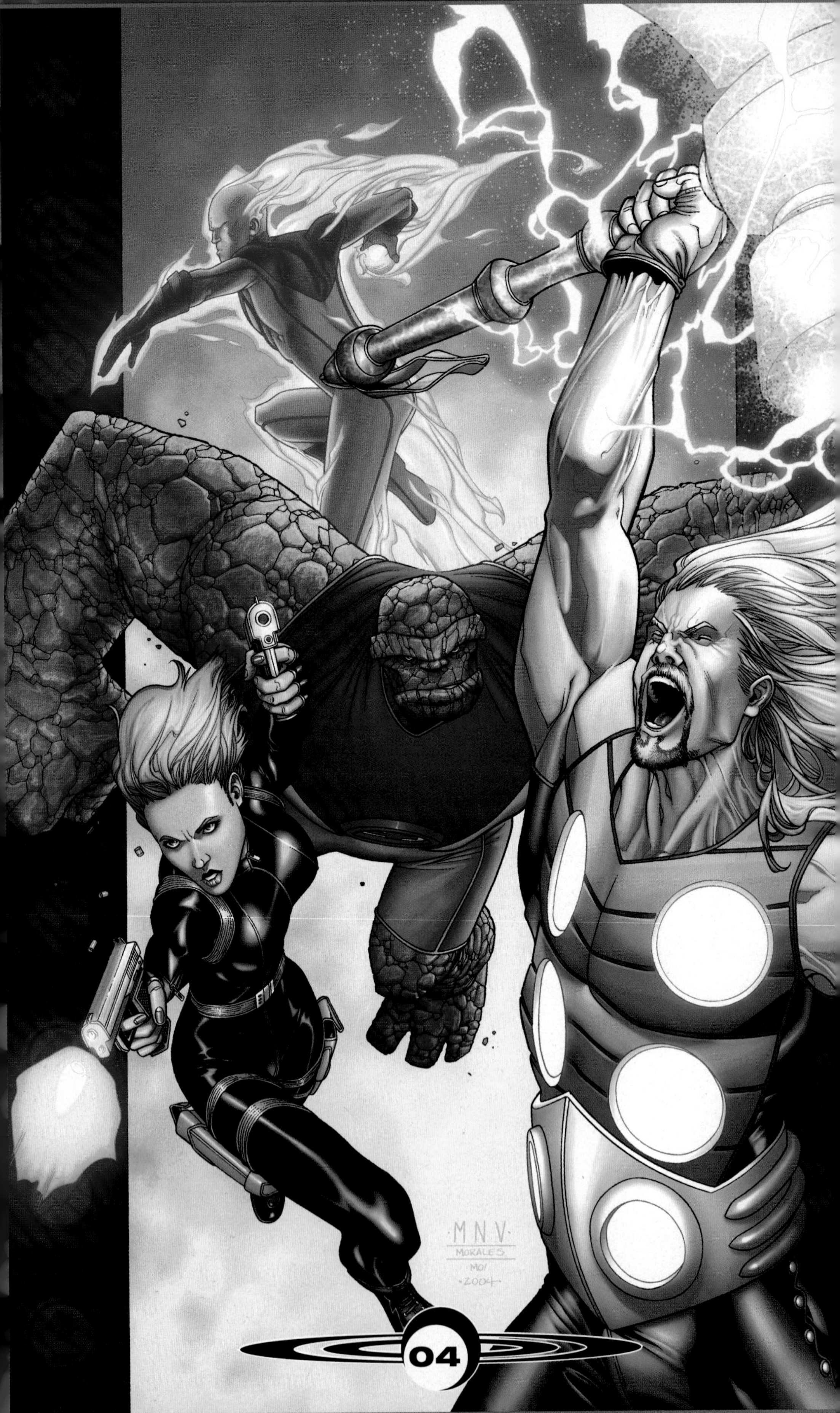
M N V
MORALES
MO!
2004

04

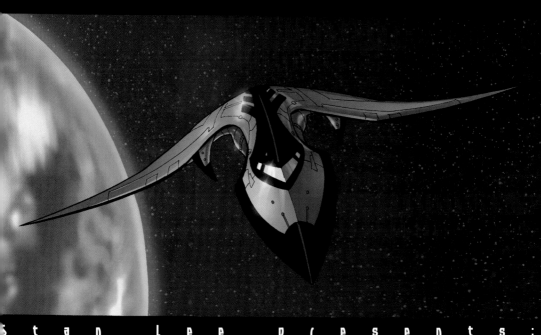

Stan Lee presents:

ULTIMATE SECRET

CHAPTER FOUR

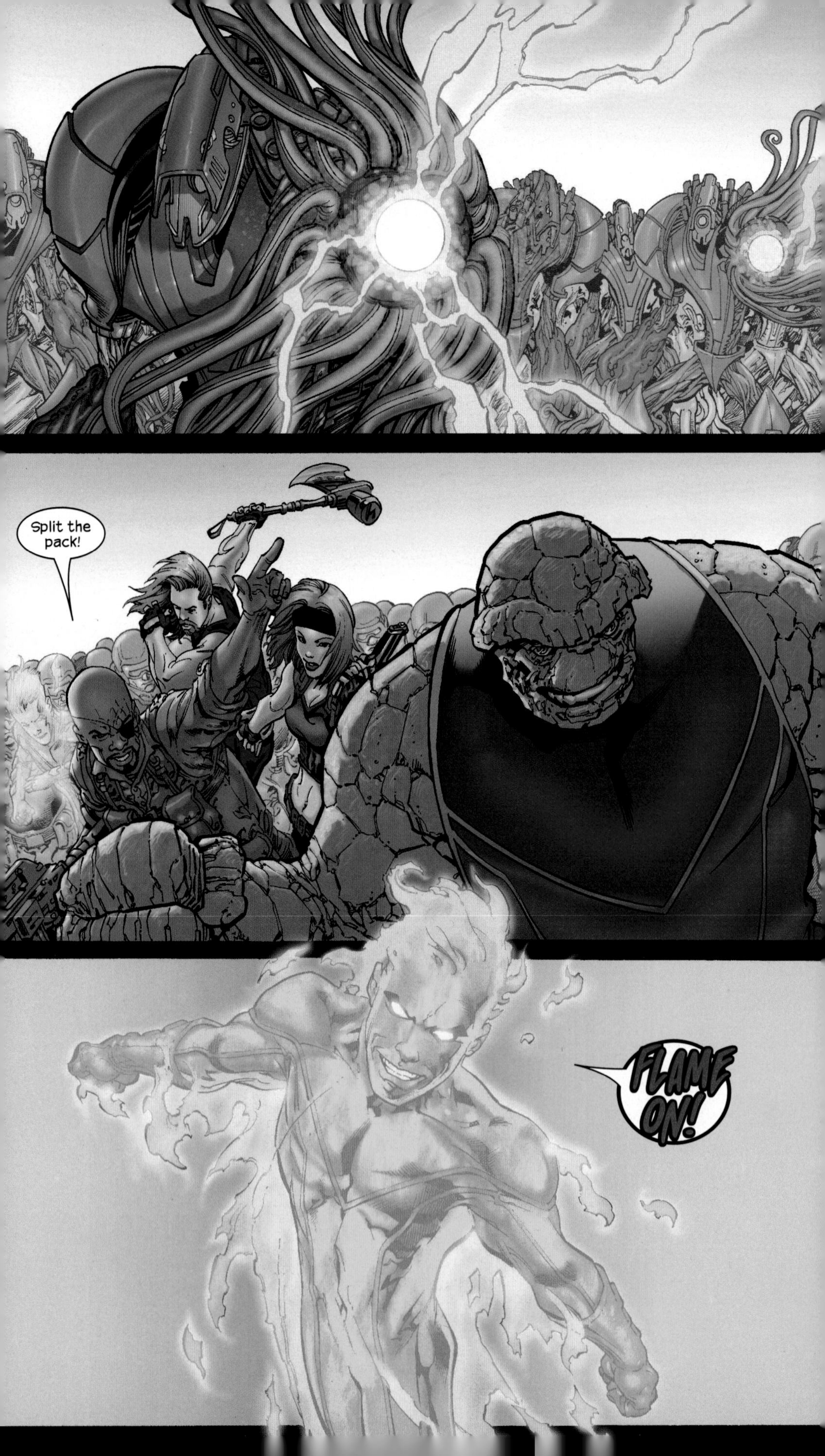
Split the pack!
FLAME ON!

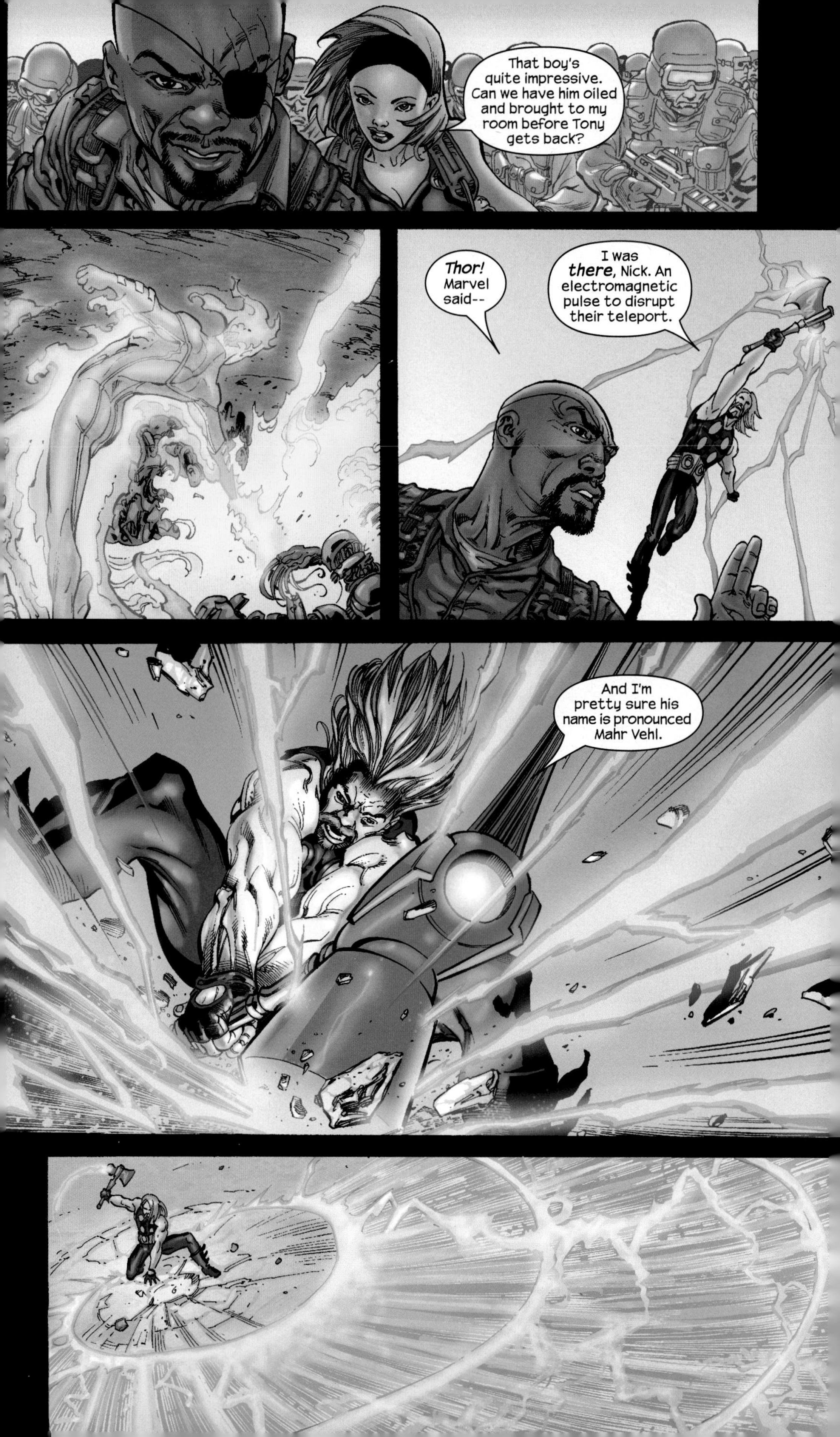
That boy's quite impressive. Can we have him oiled and brought to my room before Tony gets back?
Thor! Marvel said--
I was there, Nick. An electromagnetic pulse to disrupt their teleport.
And I'm pretty sure his name is pronounced Mahr Vehl.

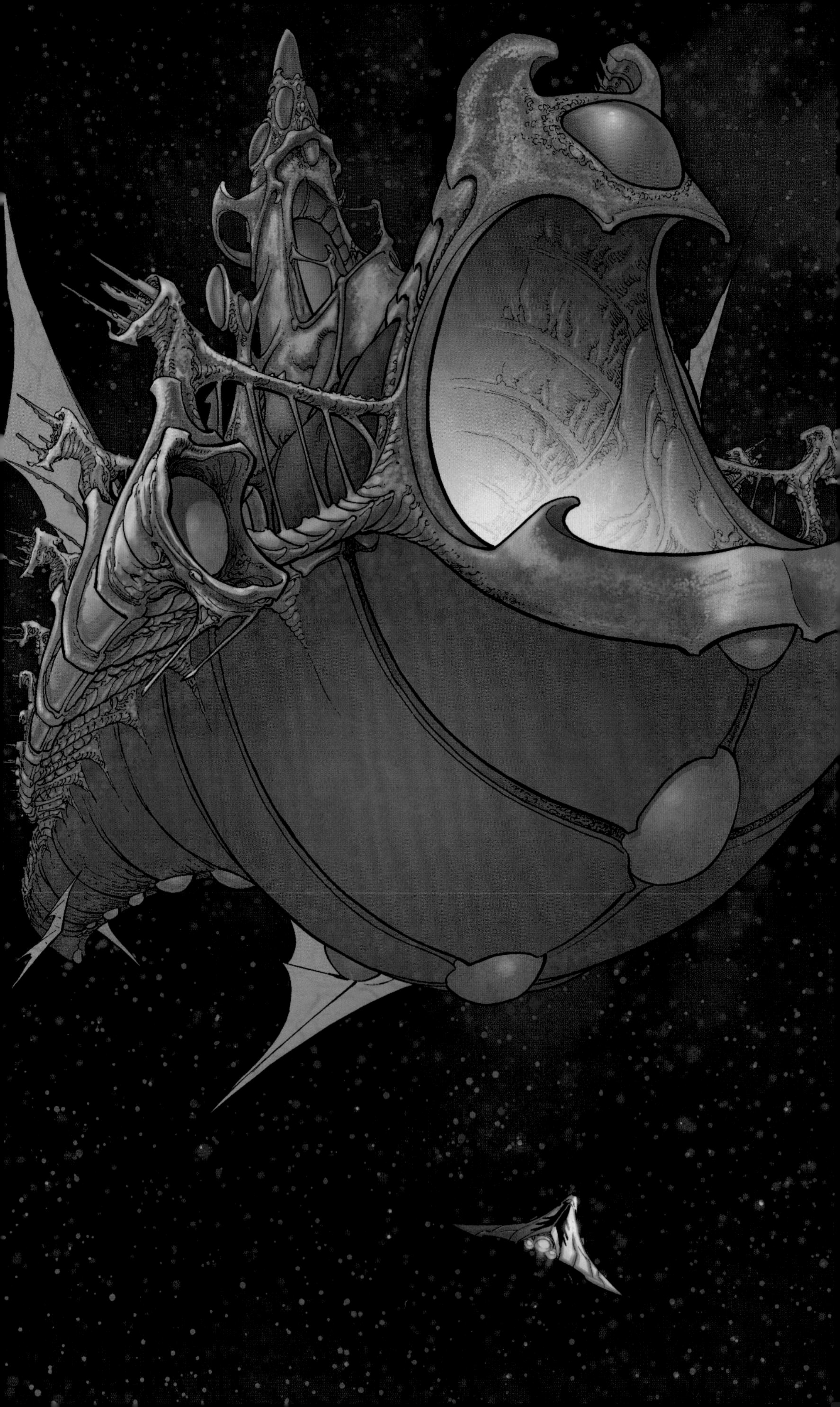

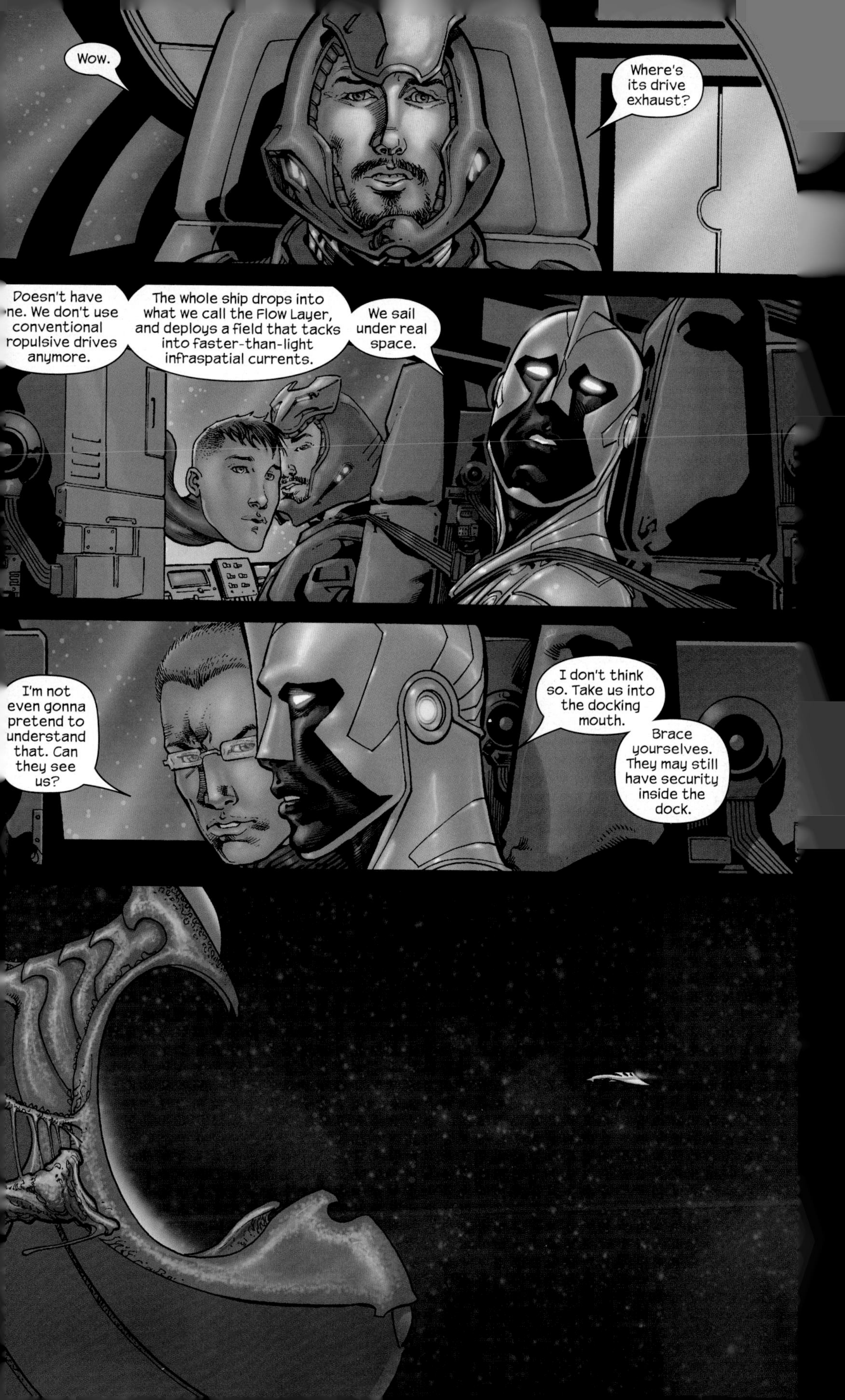
Wow.
Where's its drive exhaust?
Doesn't have ne. We don't use conventional ropulsive drives anymore.
The whole ship drops into what we call the Flow Layer, and deploys a field that tacks into faster-than-light infraspatial currents.
We sail under real space.
I'm not even gonna pretend to understand that. Can they see us?
I don't think so. Take us into the docking mouth.
Brace yourselves. They may still have security inside the dock.

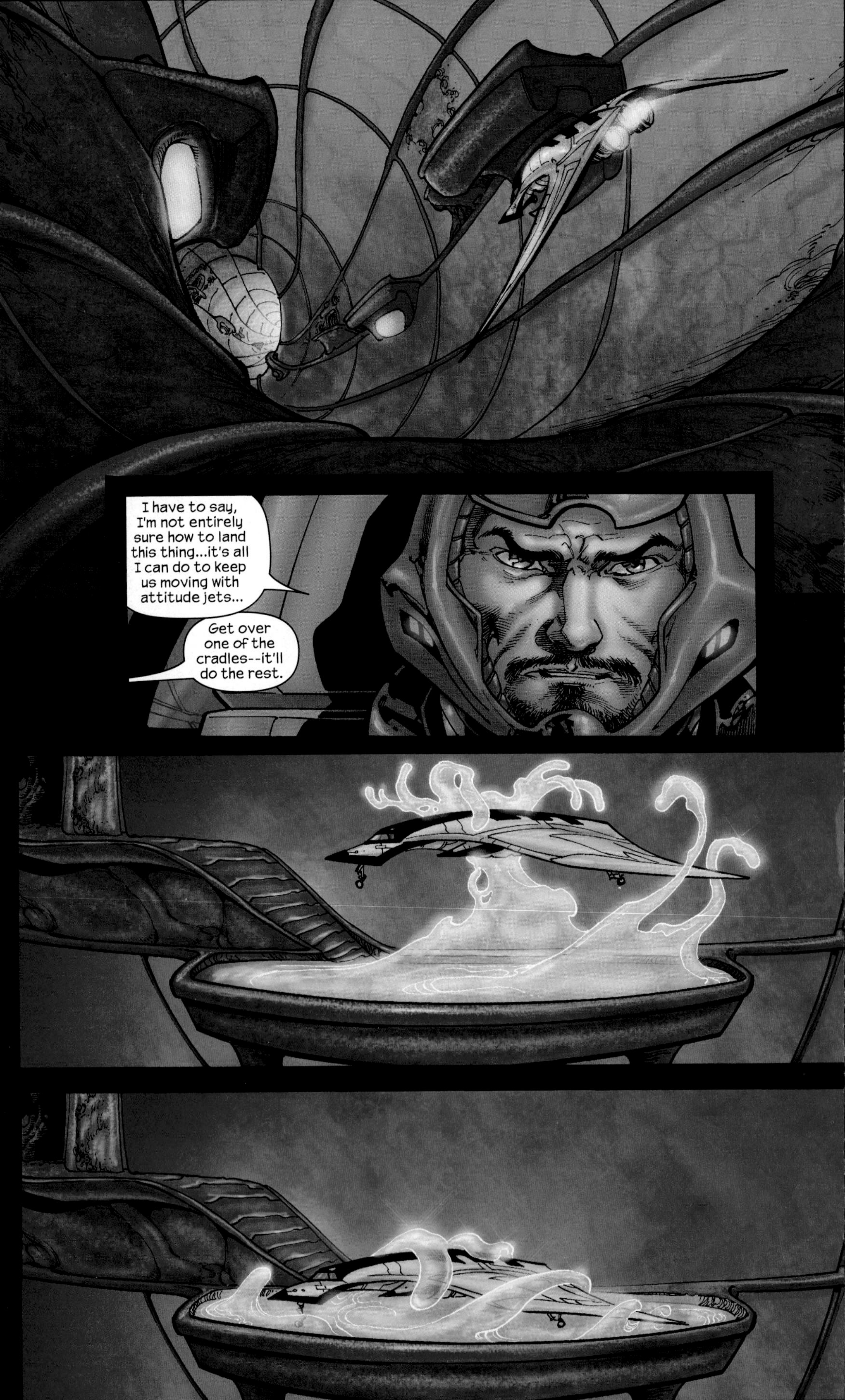

I have to say, I'm not entirely sure how to land this thing...it's all I can do to keep us moving with attitude jets...
Get over one of the cradles--it'll do the rest.

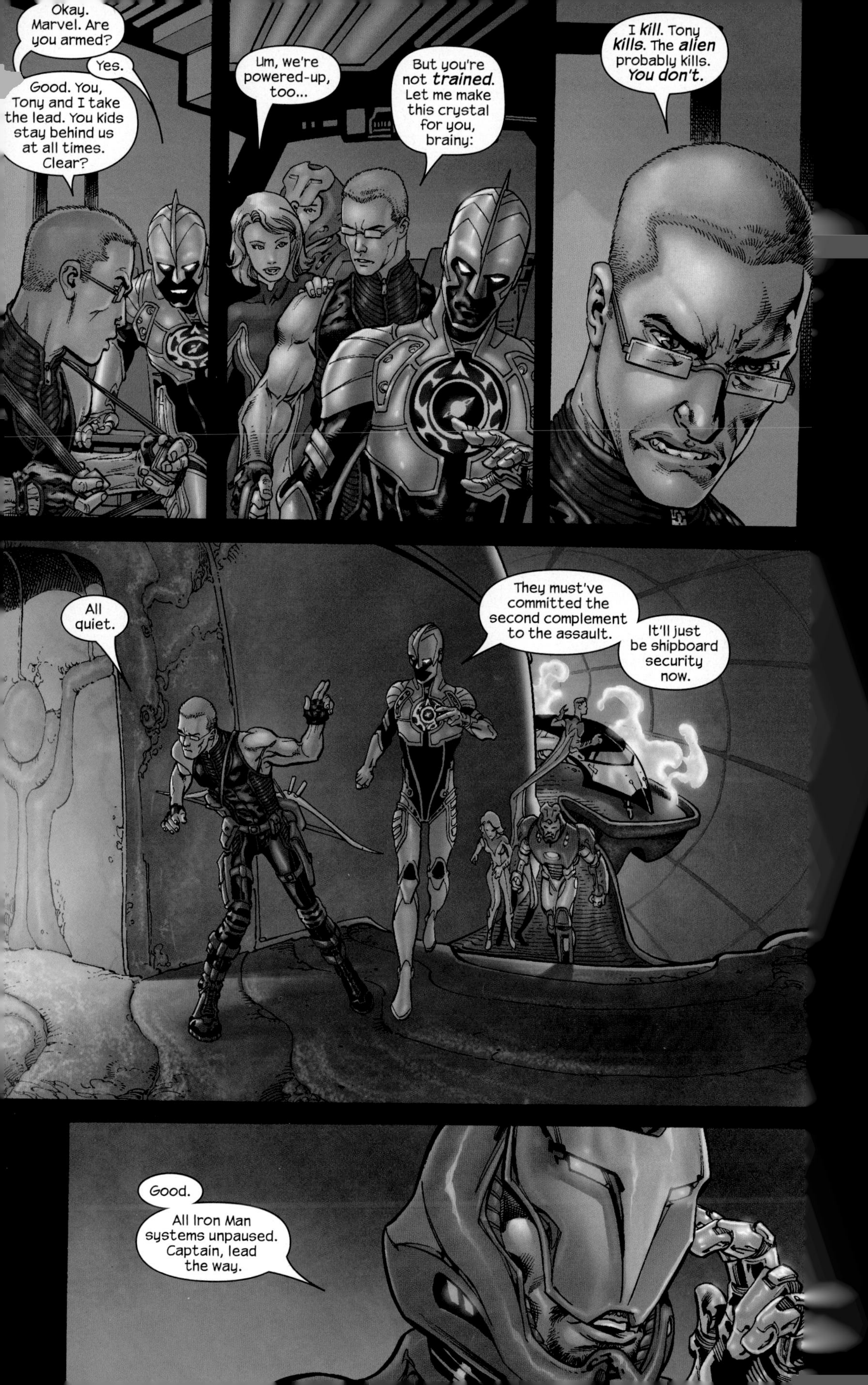
Okay. Marvel. Are you armed?
Yes.
Good. You, Tony and I take the lead. You kids stay behind us at all times. Clear?
Um, we're powered-up, too...
But you're not *trained*. Let me make this crystal for you, brainy:
I *kill*. Tony *kills*. The *alien* probably kills. *You don't.*
All quiet.
They must've committed the second complement to the assault.
It'll just be shipboard security now.
Good.
All Iron Man systems unpaused. Captain, lead the way.

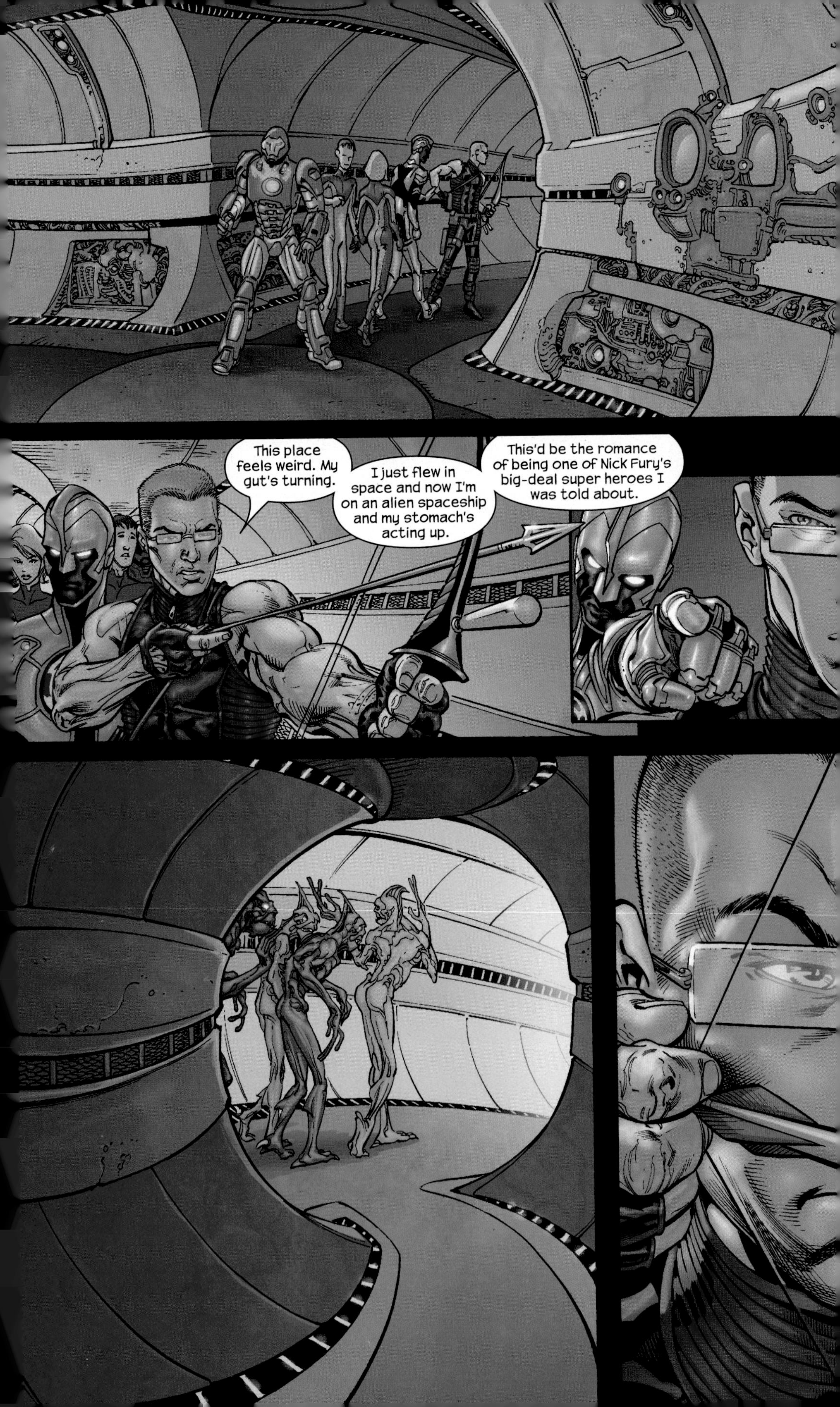
This place feels weird. My gut's turning.
I just flew in space and now I'm on an alien spaceship and my stomach's acting up.
This'd be the romance of being one of Nick Fury's big-deal super heroes I was told about.

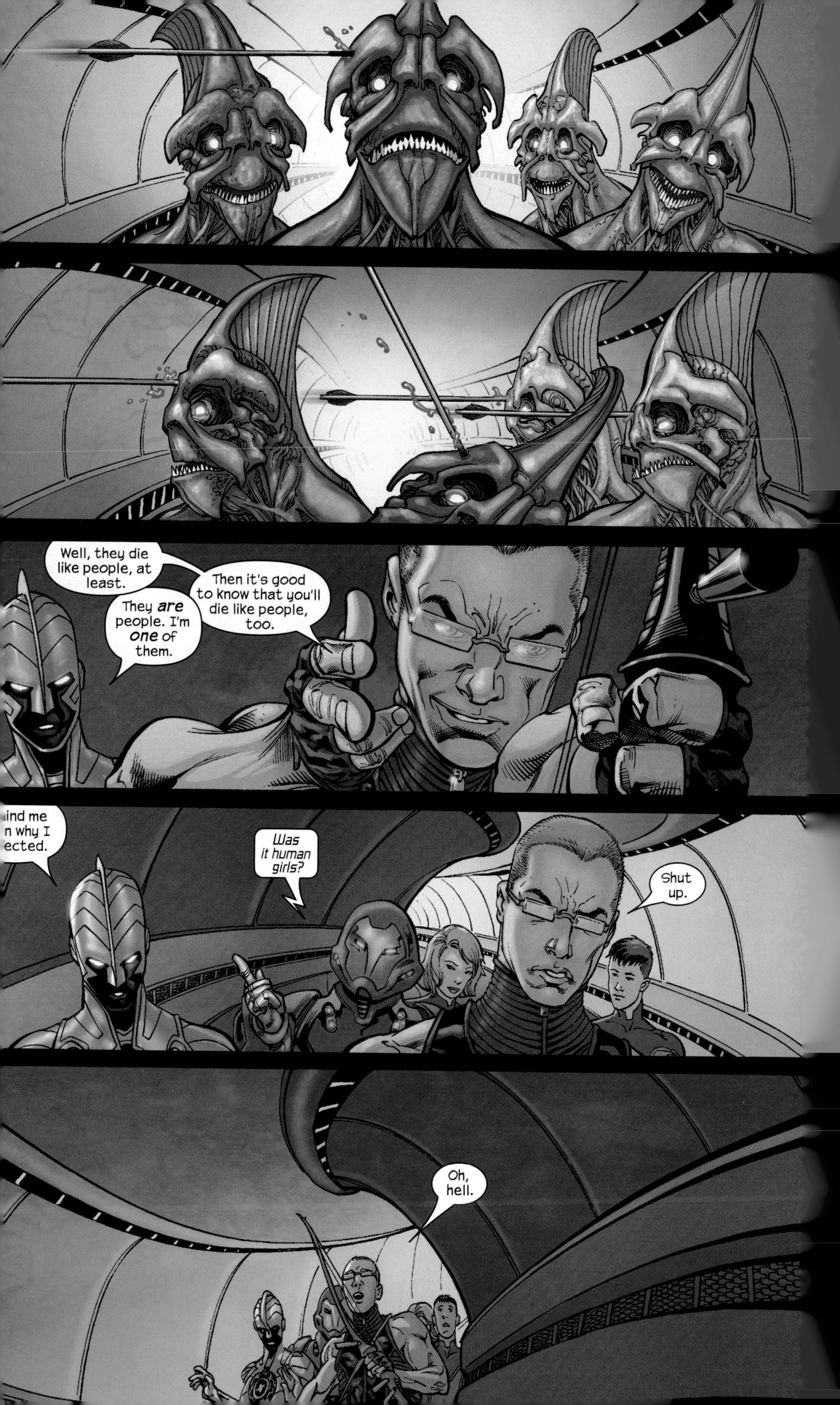

Well, they die like people, at least.
They are people. I'm one of them.
Then it's good to know that you'll die like people, too.
ind me n why I ected.
Was it human girls?
Shut up.
Oh, hell.

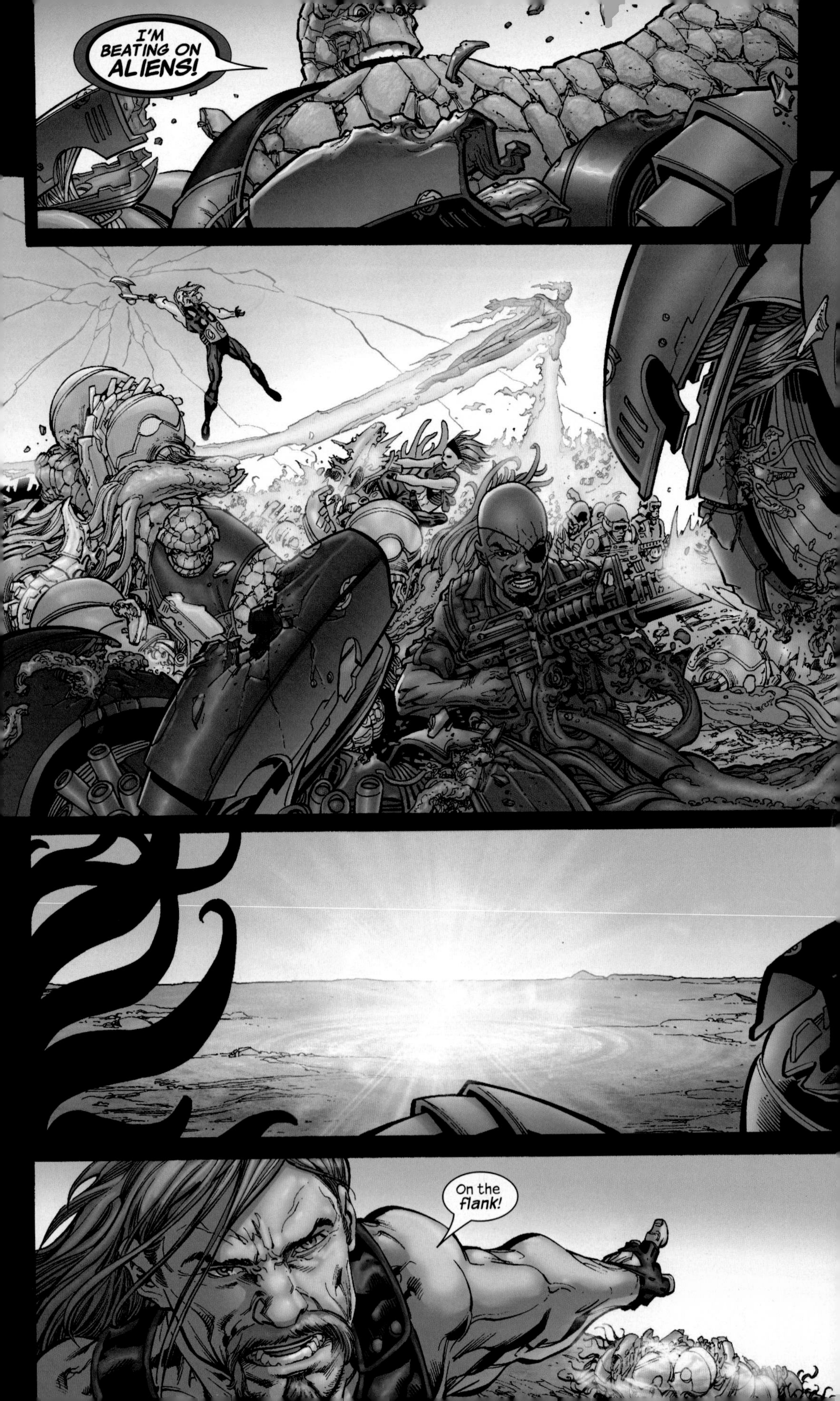
I'M BEATING ON ALIENS!
On the flank!

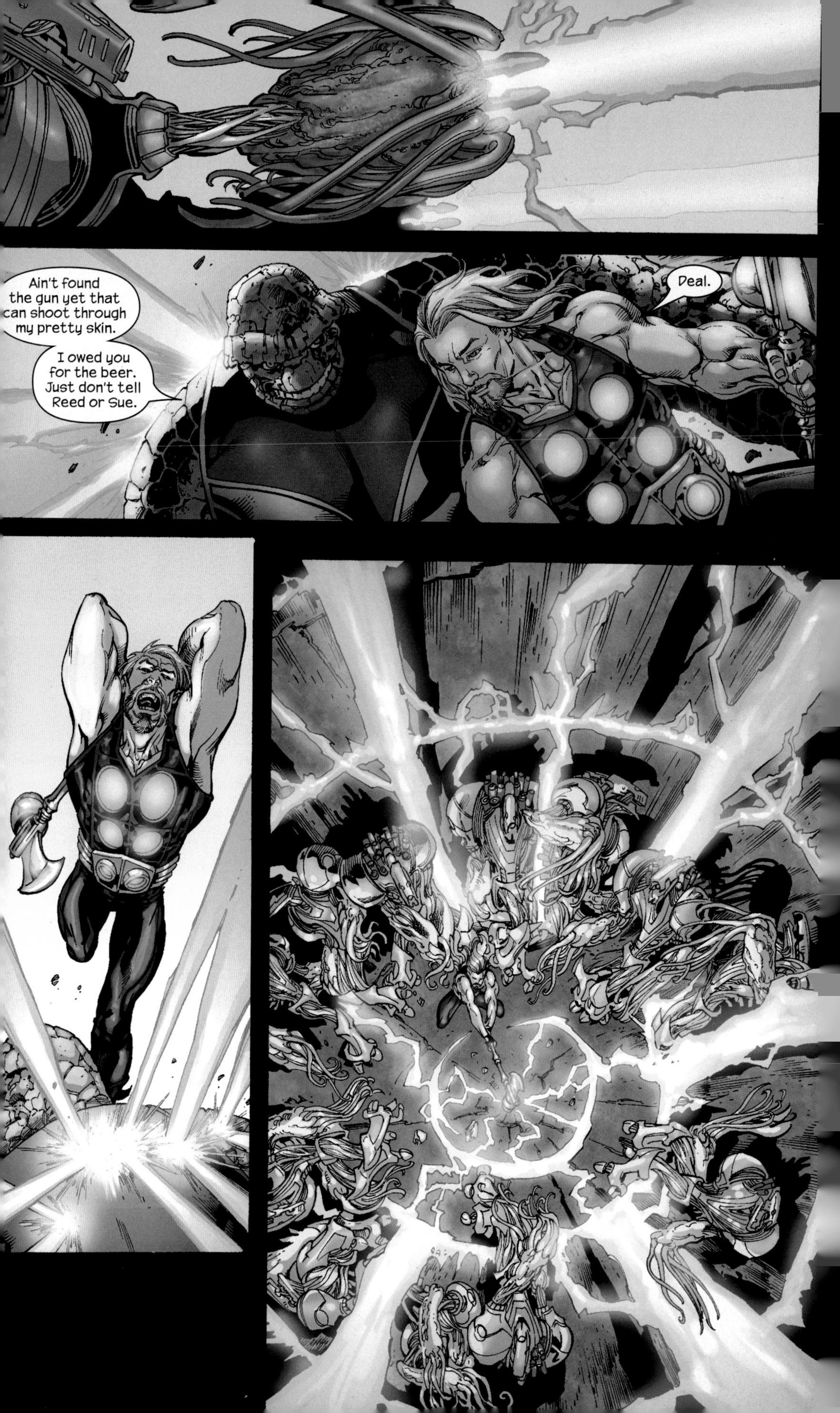
Ain't found the gun yet that can shoot through my pretty skin.
I owed you for the beer. Just don't tell Reed or Sue.
Deal.

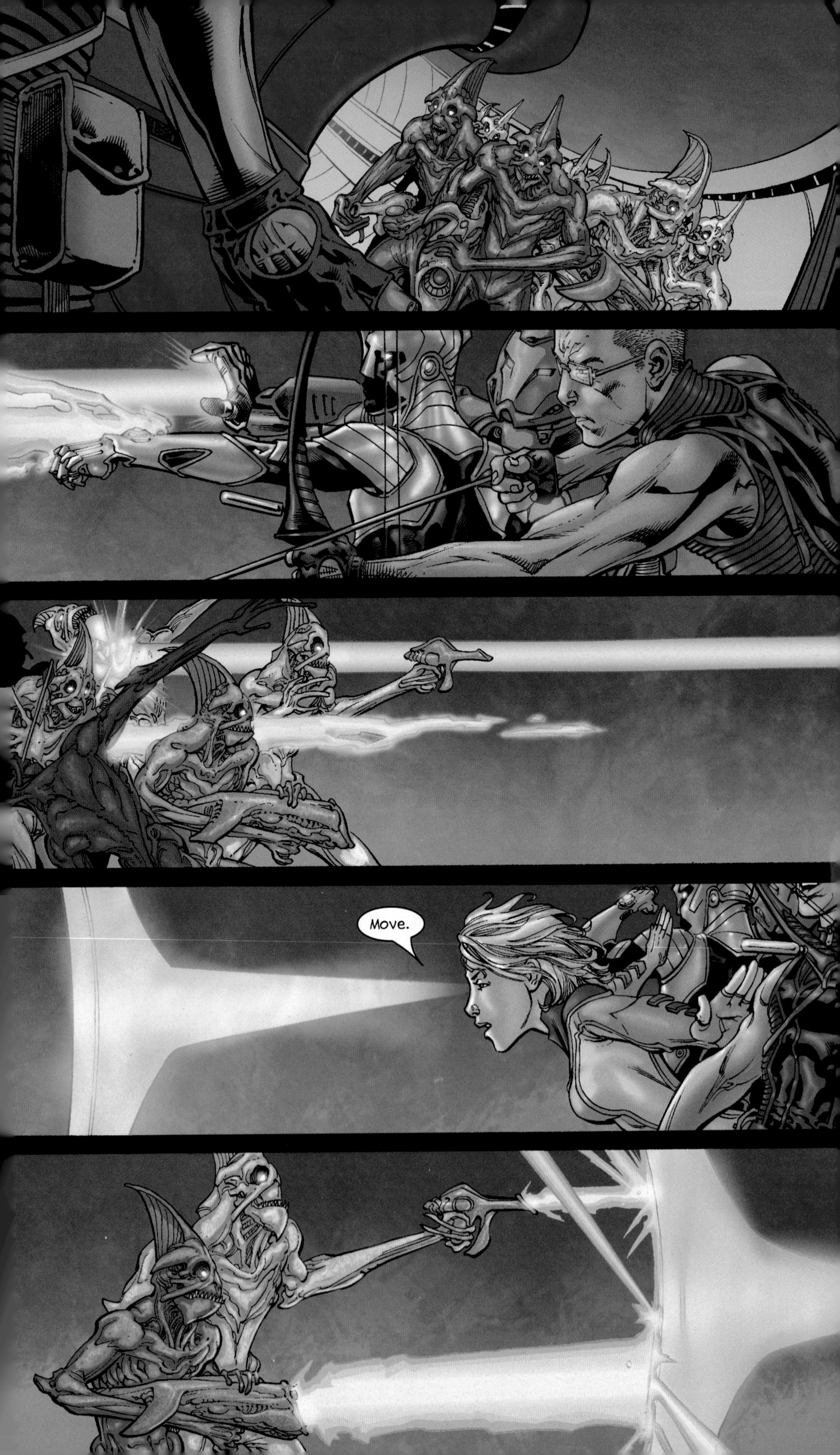
Move.

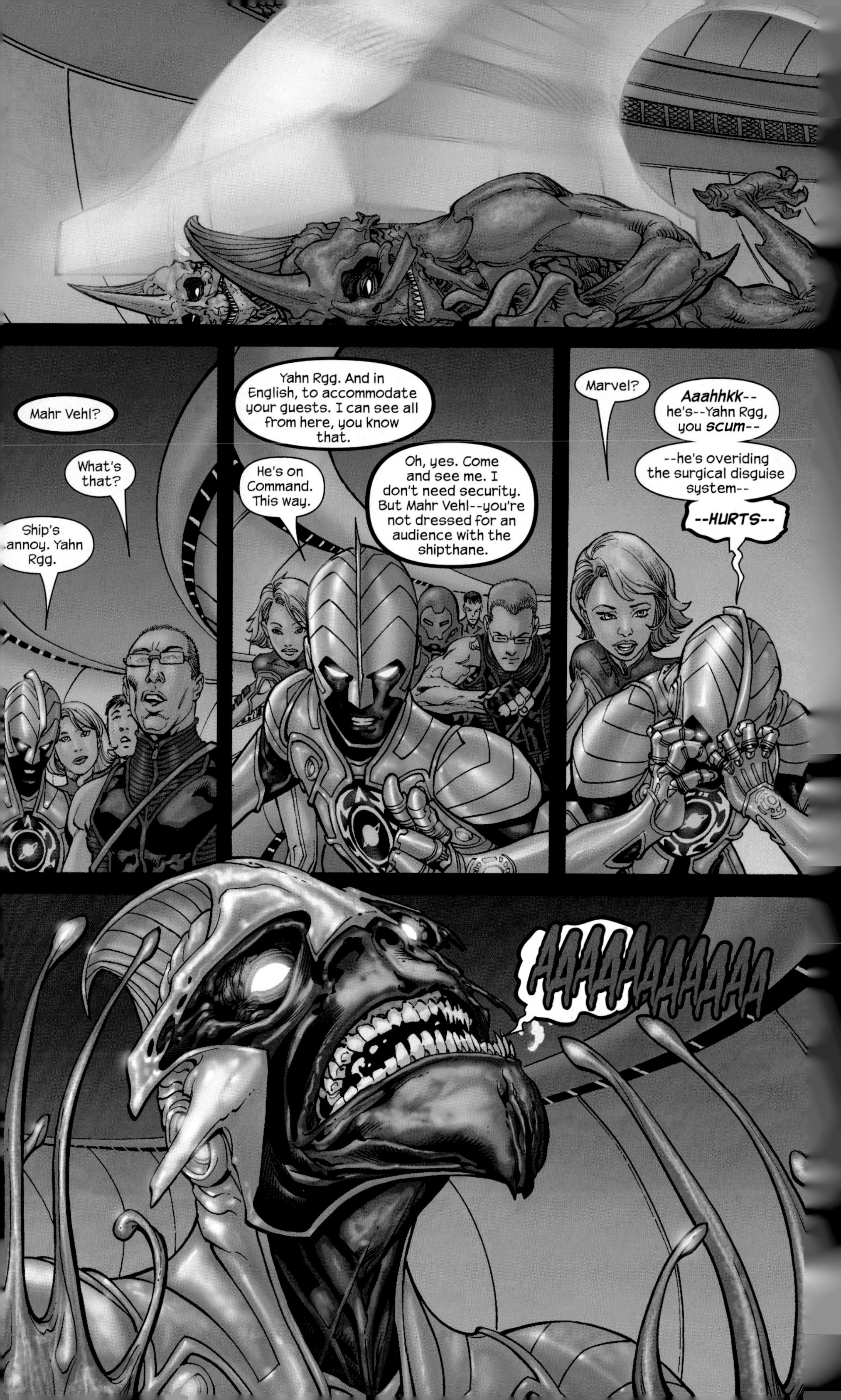
Mahr Vehl?
What's that?
Ship's annoy. Yahn Rgg.
Yahn Rgg. And in English, to accommodate your guests. I can see all from here, you know that.
He's on Command. This way.
Oh, yes. Come and see me. I don't need security. But Mahr Vehl--you're not dressed for an audience with the shipthane.
Marvel?
Aaahhkk-- he's--Yahn Rgg, you scum--
--he's overiding the surgical disguise system--
--HURTS--
AAAAAAAAAAA

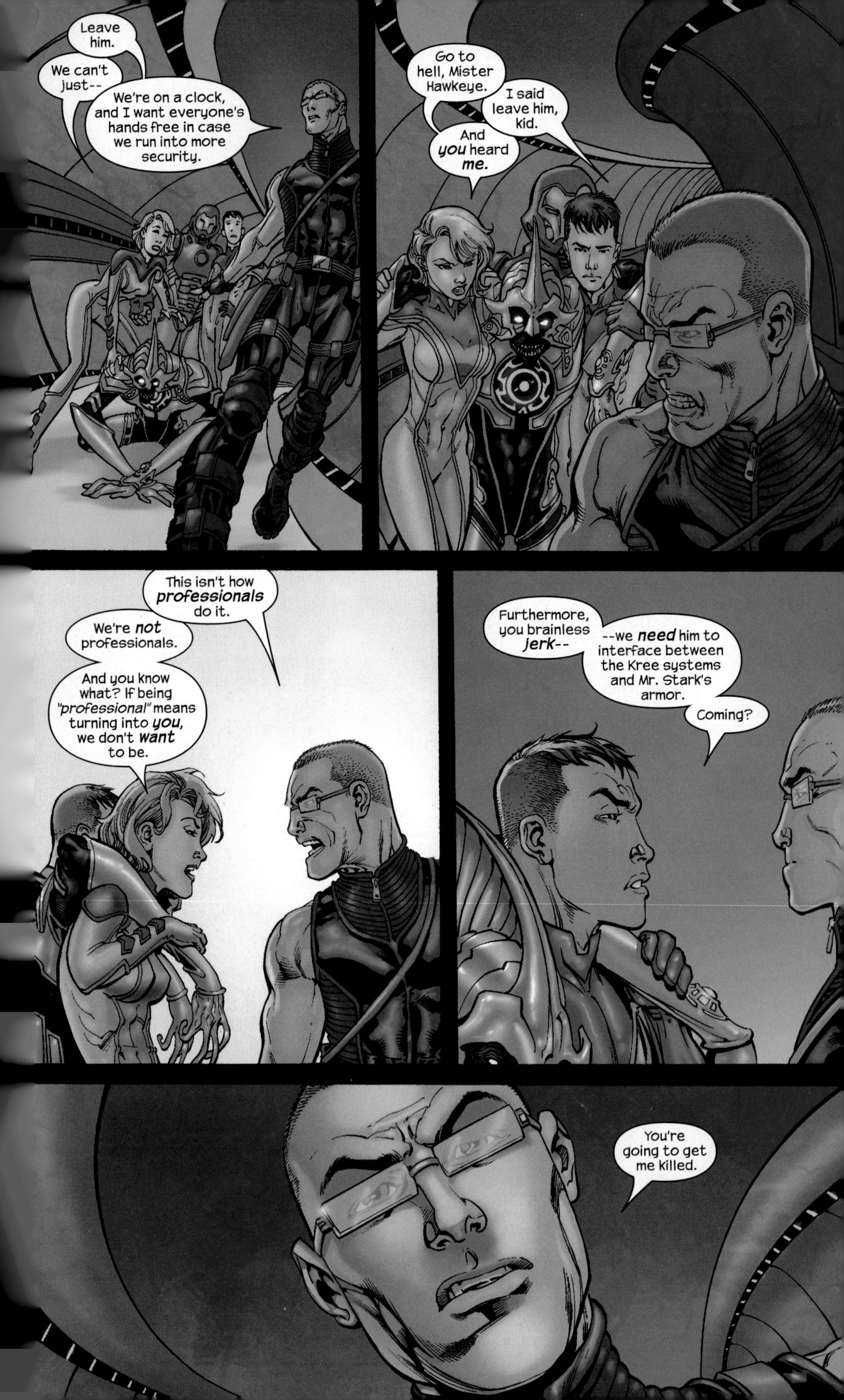
Leave him.
We can't just--
We're on a clock, and I want everyone's hands free in case we run into more security.
Go to hell, Mister Hawkeye.
I said leave him, kid.
And *you* heard *me.*
This isn't how *professionals* do it.
We're *not* professionals.
And you know what? If being *"professional"* means turning into *you*, we don't *want* to be.
Furthermore, you brainless *jerk*--
--we *need* him to interface between the Kree systems and Mr. Stark's armor.
Coming?
You're going to get me killed.

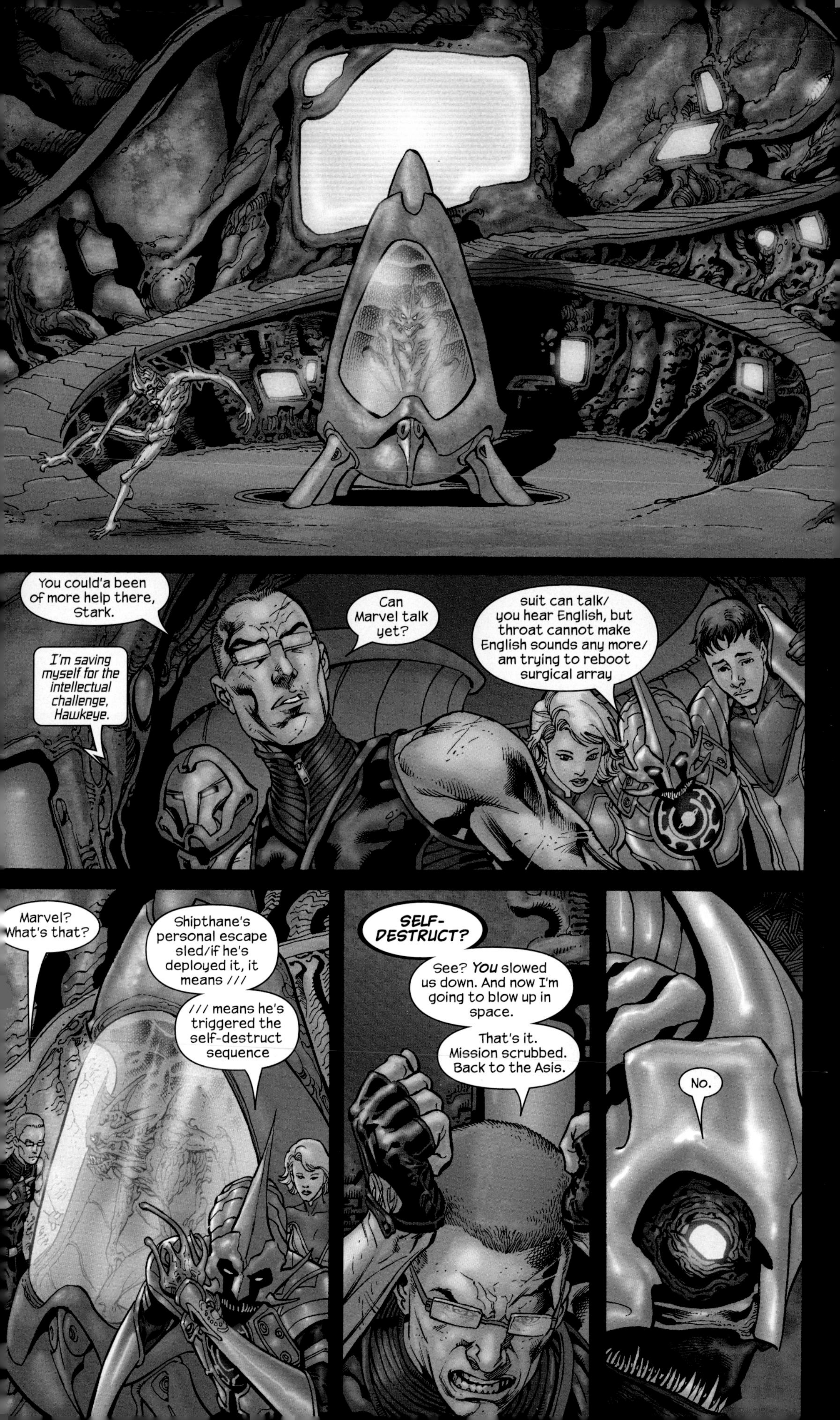
You could'a been of more help there, Stark.
I'm saving myself for the intellectual challenge, Hawkeye.
Can Marvel talk yet?
suit can talk/ you hear English, but throat cannot make English sounds any more/ am trying to reboot surgical array
Marvel? What's that?
Shipthane's personal escape sled/if he's deployed it, it means ///
/// means he's triggered the self-destruct sequence
SELF-DESTRUCT?
See? YOU slowed us down. And now I'm going to blow up in space.
That's it. Mission scrubbed. Back to the Asis.
No.

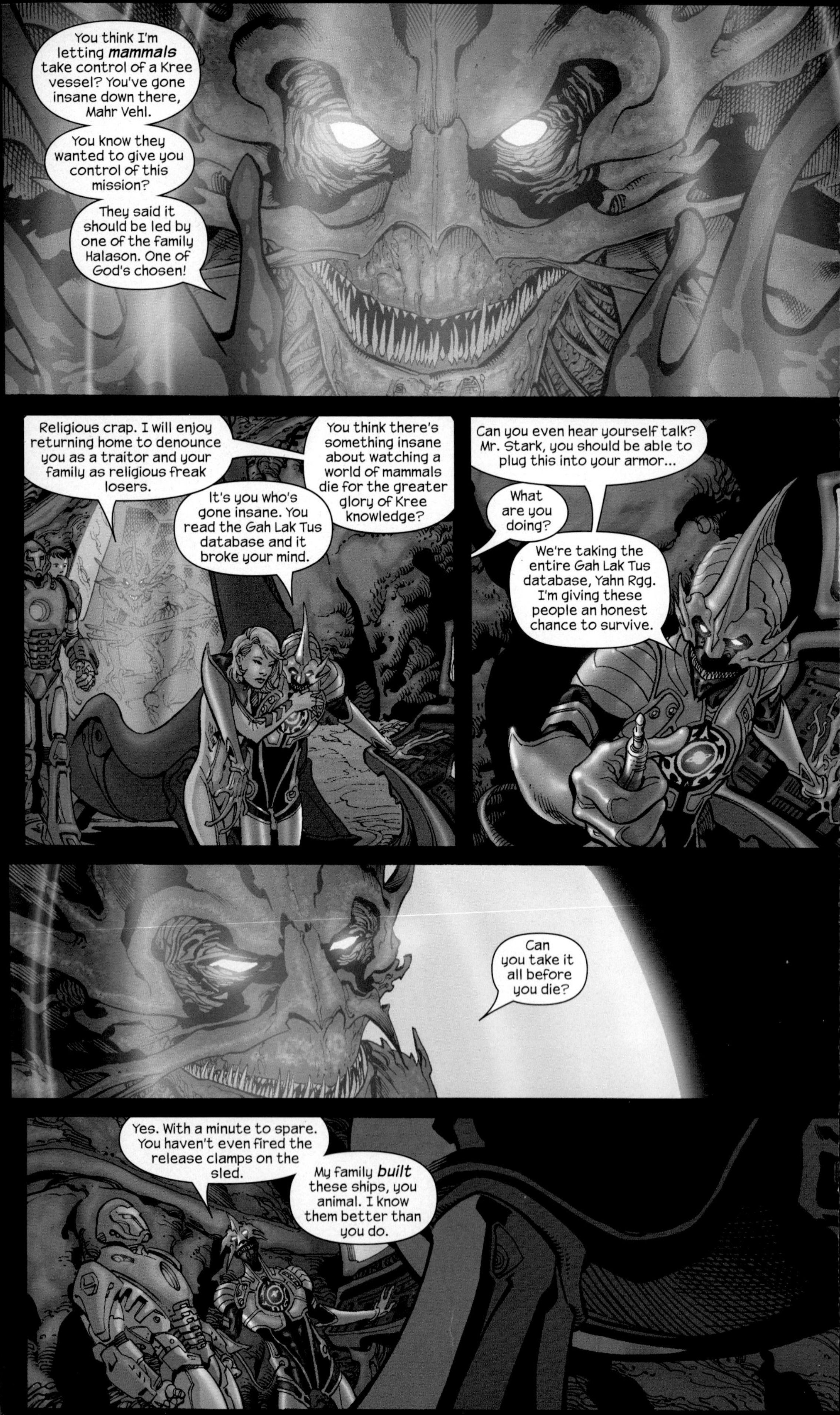
You think I'm letting **mammals** take control of a Kree vessel? You've gone insane down there, Mahr Vehl.
You know they wanted to give you control of this mission?
They said it should be led by one of the family Halason. One of God's chosen!
Religious crap. I will enjoy returning home to denounce you as a traitor and your family as religious freak losers.
You think there's something insane about watching a world of mammals die for the greater glory of Kree knowledge?
It's you who's gone insane. You read the Gah Lak Tus database and it broke your mind.
Can you even hear yourself talk? Mr. Stark, you should be able to plug this into your armor...
What are you doing?
We're taking the entire Gah Lak Tus database, Yahn Rgg. I'm giving these people an honest chance to survive.
Can you take it all before you die?
Yes. With a minute to spare. You haven't even fired the release clamps on the sled.
My family **built** these ships, you animal. I know them better than you do.

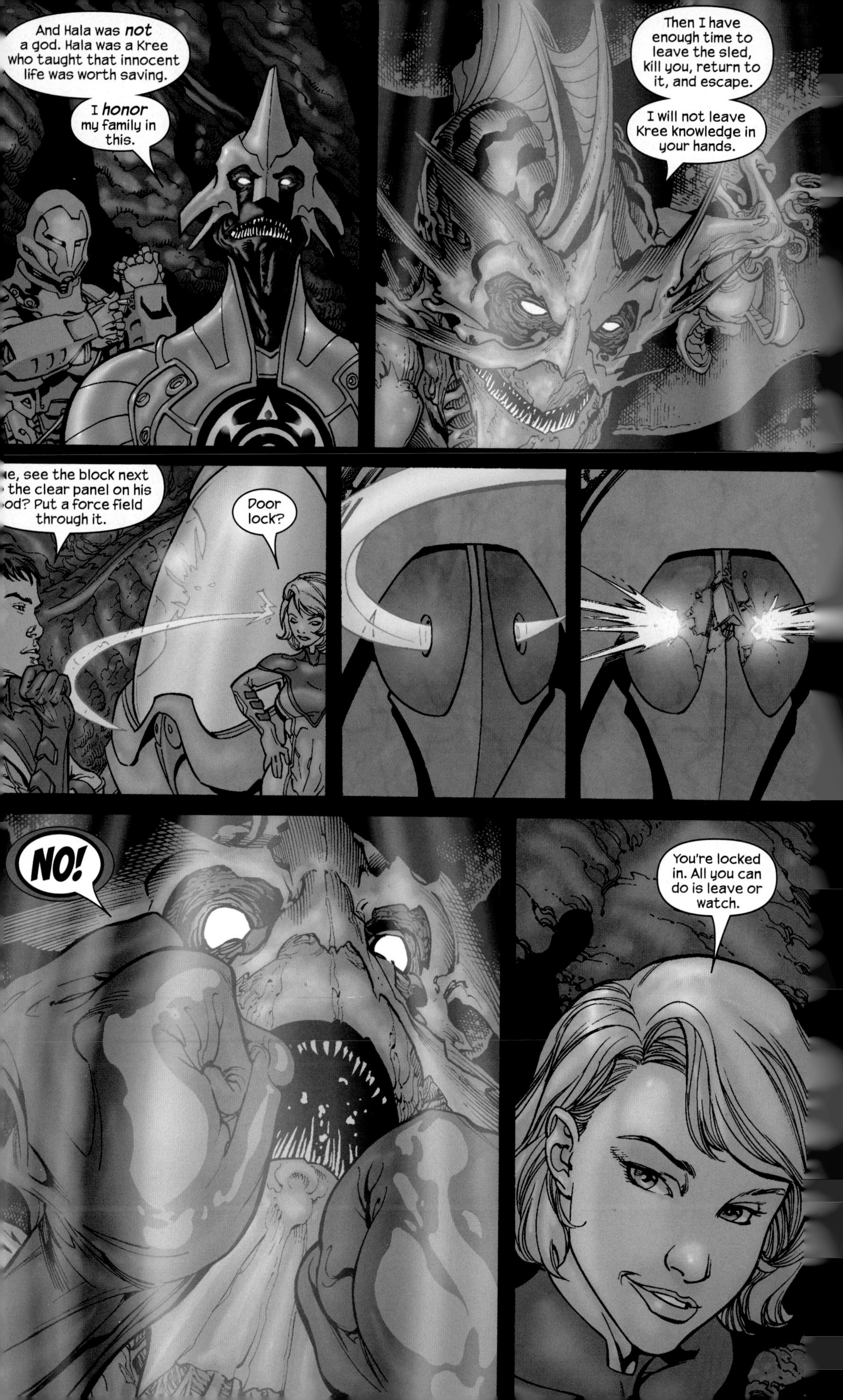
And Hala was not a god. Hala was a Kree who taught that innocent life was worth saving.
I honor my family in this.
Then I have enough time to leave the sled, kill you, return to it, and escape.
I will not leave Kree knowledge in your hands.
e, see the block next the clear panel on his od? Put a force field through it.
Door lock?
NO!
You're locked in. All you can do is leave or watch.

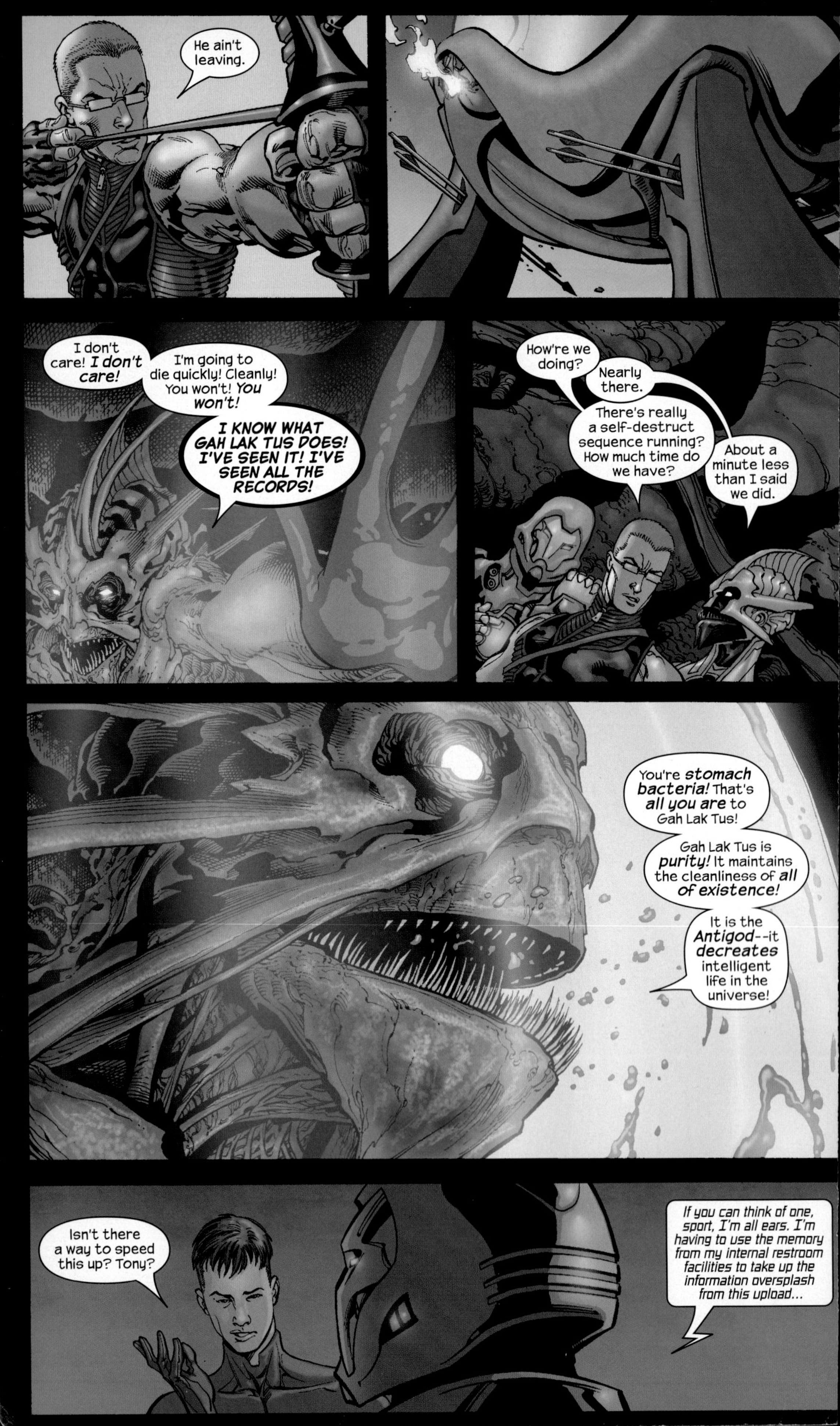

He ain't leaving.
I don't care! *I don't care!*
I'm going to die quickly! Cleanly! You won't! *You won't!*
I KNOW WHAT GAH LAK TUS DOES! I'VE SEEN IT! I'VE SEEN ALL THE RECORDS!
How're we doing?
Nearly there.
There's really a self-destruct sequence running? How much time do we have?
About a minute less than I said we did.
You're ***stomach bacteria!*** That's ***all you are*** to Gah Lak Tus!
Gah Lak Tus is ***purity!*** It maintains the cleanliness of ***all of existence!***
It is the ***Antigod***--it ***decreates*** intelligent life in the universe!
Isn't there a way to speed this up? Tony?
If you can think of one, sport, I'm all ears. I'm having to use the memory from my internal restroom facilities to take up the information oversplash from this upload...

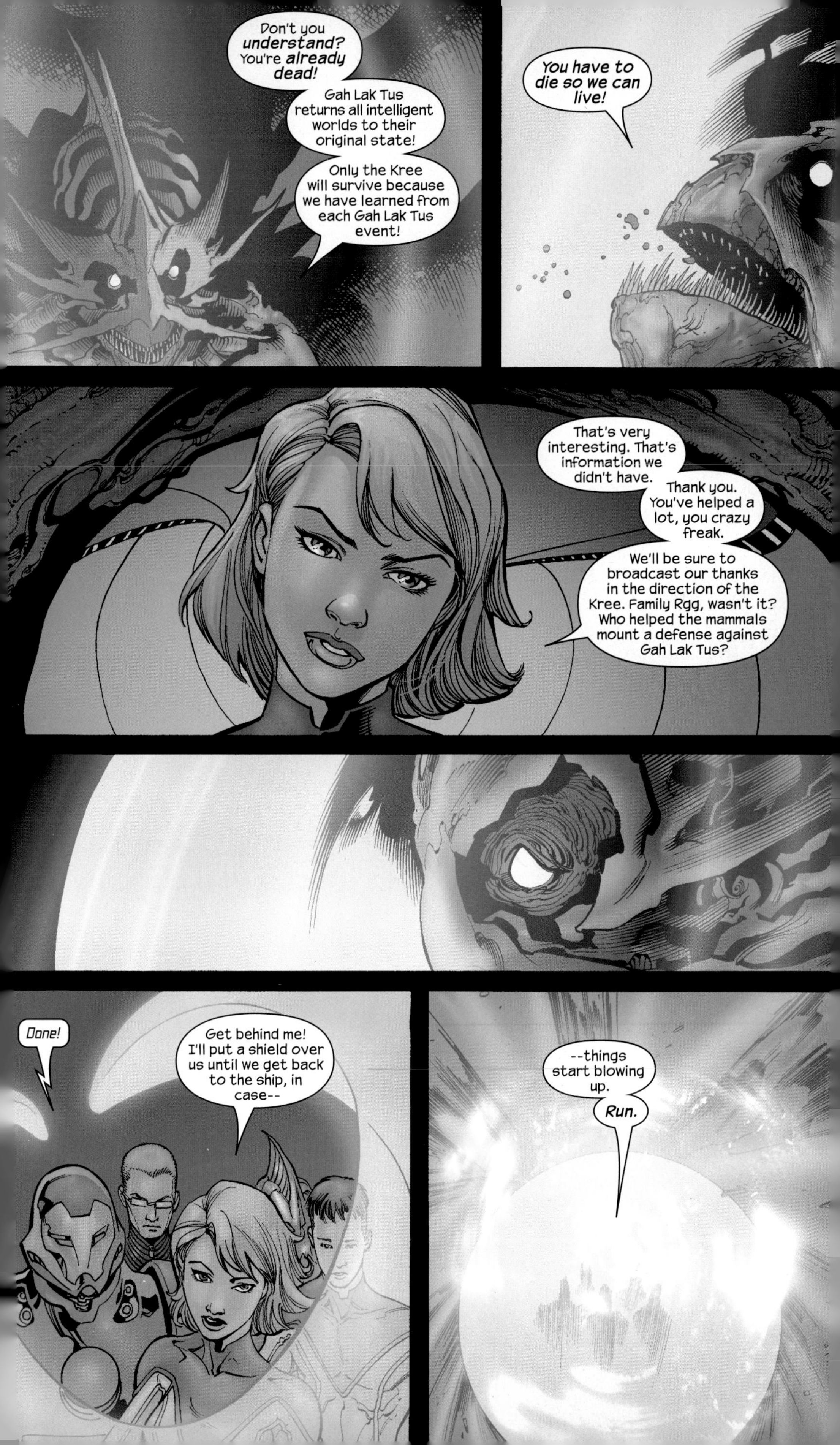
Don't you understand? You're already dead!
Gah Lak Tus returns all intelligent worlds to their original state!
Only the Kree will survive because we have learned from each Gah Lak Tus event!
You have to die so we can live!
That's very interesting. That's information we didn't have.
Thank you. You've helped a lot, you crazy freak.
We'll be sure to broadcast our thanks in the direction of the Kree. Family Rgg, wasn't it? Who helped the mammals mount a defense against Gah Lak Tus?
Done!
Get behind me! I'll put a shield over us until we get back to the ship, in case--
--things start blowing up.
Run.

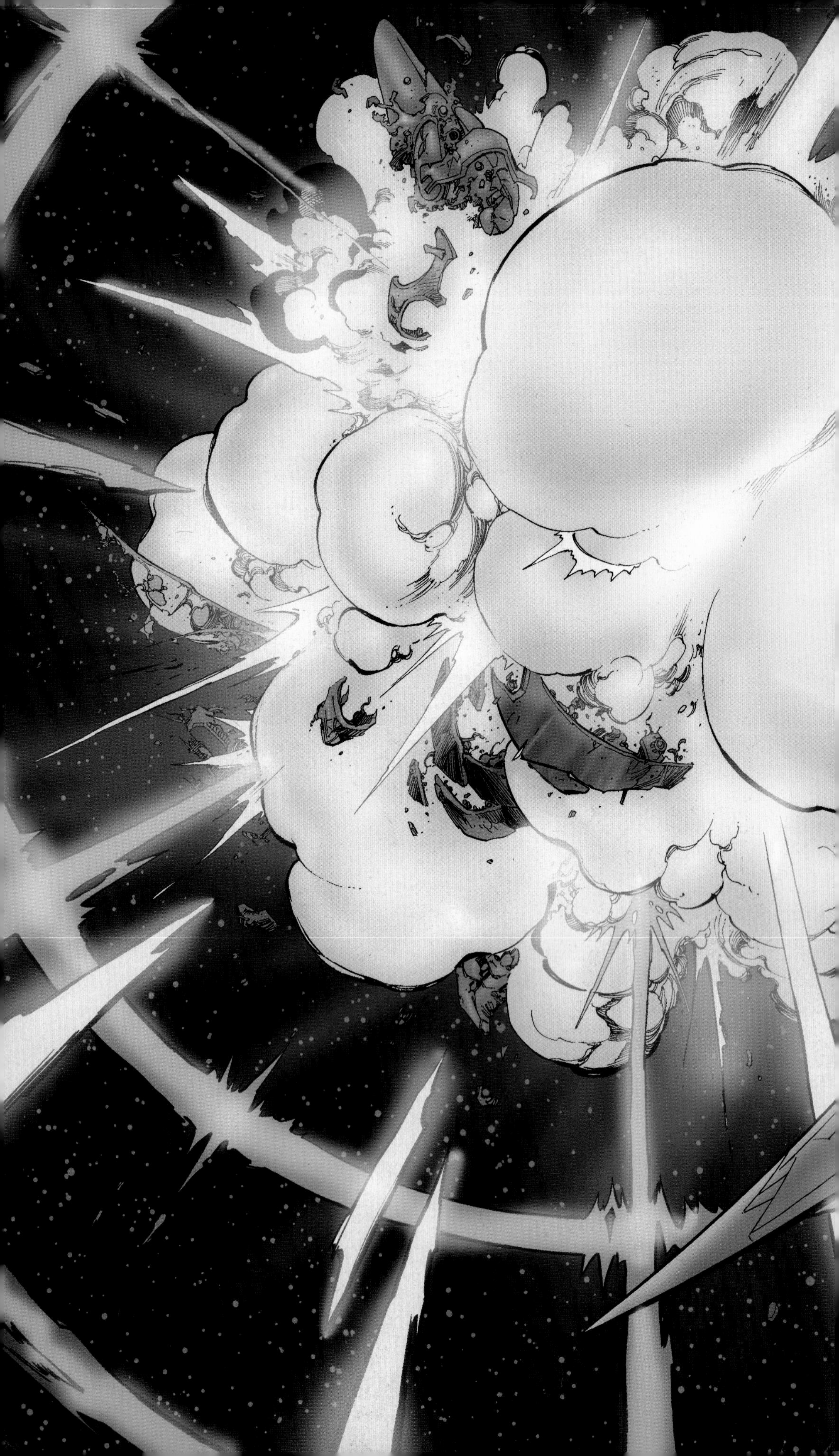

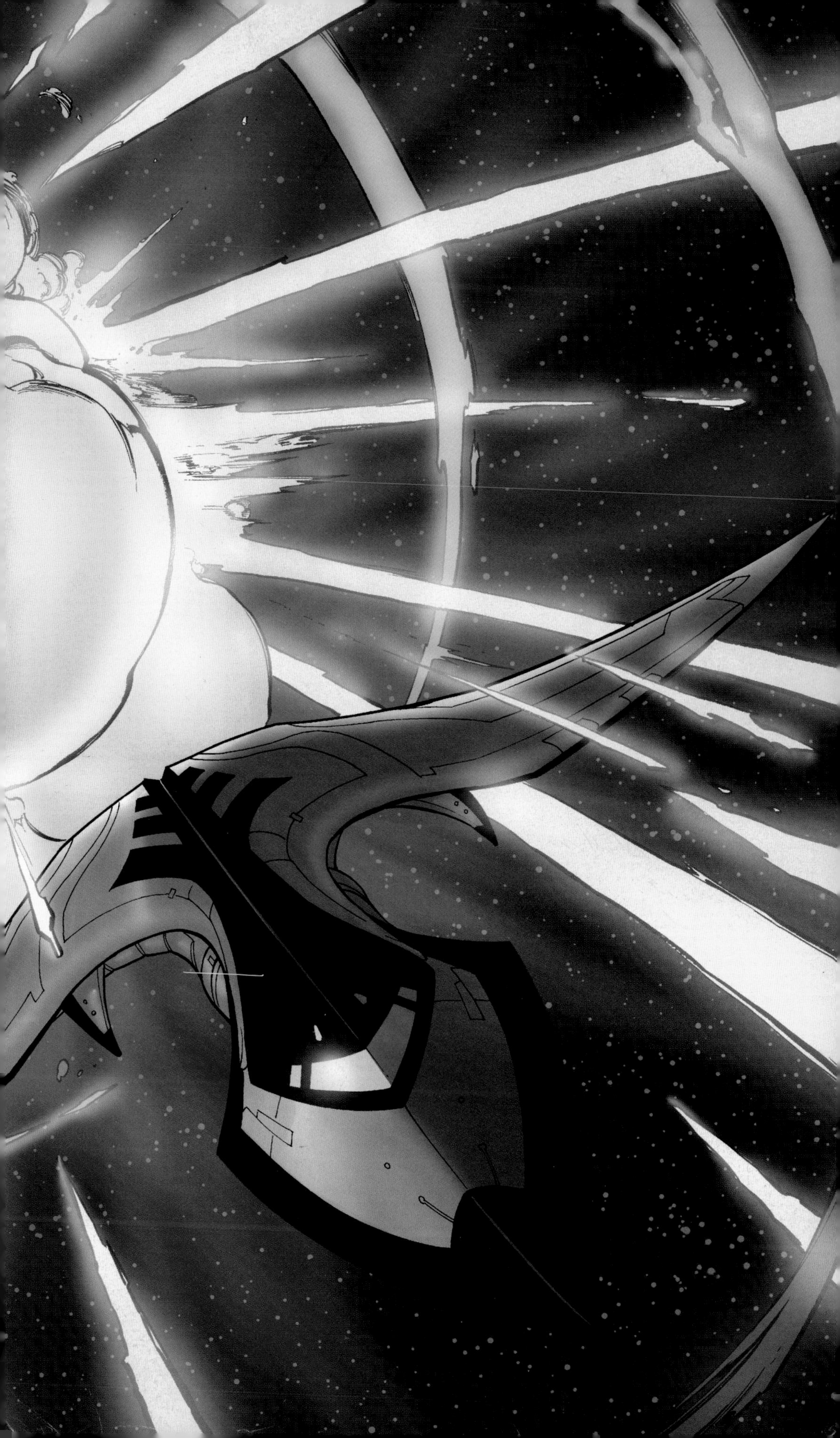

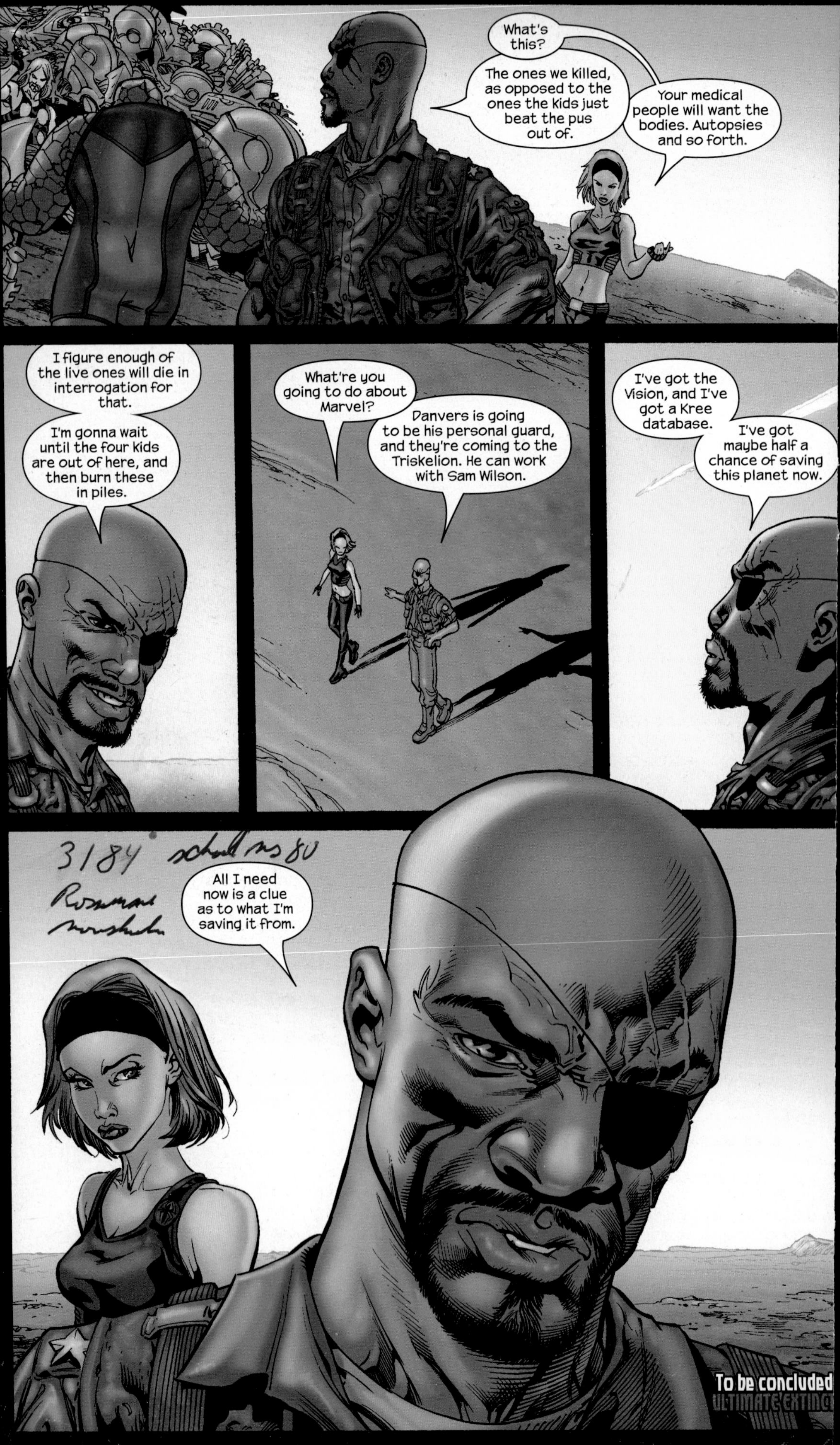
What's this?
The ones we killed, as opposed to the ones the kids just beat the pus out of.
Your medical people will want the bodies. Autopsies and so forth.
I figure enough of the live ones will die in interrogation for that.
I'm gonna wait until the four kids are out of here, and then burn these in piles.
What're you going to do about Marvel?
Danvers is going to be his personal guard, and they're coming to the Triskelion. He can work with Sam Wilson.
I've got the Vision, and I've got a Kree database.
I've got maybe half a chance of saving this planet now.
All I need now is a clue as to what I'm saving it from.
To be concluded
ULTIMATE EXTINCT